Renée Phillips sounds the clarion call for self-empowerment and is the voice to the artist of the 21st century.
Bernard Olshan: Artist, National Academy; Vice President, American Society of Contemporary Artists; and Vice President, New York Artists Equity

Success Now! For Artists

A Motivational Guide For the Artrepreneur

RENÉE PHILLIPS

Manhattan Arts
INTERNATIONAL

Success Now! For Artists
A Motivational Guide For the Artrepreneur

Copyright © Renée Phillips, Manhattan Arts International, 1991, 1992, 1993, 1994, 1995, 1996, 1997, 1998, 1999.
All rights reserved. No part of this book may be reproduced or utilized in any form or by any means, electronic or mechanical, including photocopying, recording, or by any information storage or retrieval system, without written permission from the author, except by a reviewer, who may quote brief passages in a review.

Published by Manhattan Arts International
200 East 72 Street, Suite 26L, New York, NY 10021
Tel: (212) 472-1660
Fax: (212) 794-0324
Email: Manarts@aol.com

Manhattan Arts International is also the publisher of
New York Contemporary Art Galleries: The Complete Annual Guide,
Presentation Power Tools For Fine Artists,
Manhattan Arts International magazine, and
Success Now! For Artists: The Artrepreneur Newsletter for Fine Artists

Success Now! For Artists
A Motivational Guide For the Artrepreneur
Library of Congress Catalog Card Number: 97-75488
ISBN 0-9646358-6-0
First Edition

Printed in the United States of America
by Morris Publishing, Kearney, NE

Dedication

This book is dedicated to every artist who knows that being an artist is a life force, not a career choice.

Acknowledgments

This book would not exist without the encouragement I have received from the artists and artists' agents who have attended my seminars and sought my counseling, and from all of the creative individuals who have shared their dreams and accomplishments with me.

The process of creating this book was a joyful team effort. I sincerely thank Judy Herczfeld Hoffmannn, for her editorial assistance. And, I appreciate the creative advice from Gaye Elise Beda and Roy Tiesler regarding the book's cover.

A wealth of gratitude goes to so many friends and colleagues who endorsed this book from its inception and contributed their quotes, including Sidney H. Hermel, Artist and President of the Pastel Society of America, Lynne Friedman, Artist and President of New York Society of Women Artists, Donna Marxer, Artist and Executive Director of Artists Talk on Art, Bernard Olshan, Artist and Vice-President of the American Society of Contemporary Artists, Edward Rubin, New York Art Writer and Critic, and Regina Stewart, Artist and Executive Director of New York Artists Equity Association.

A warm appreciation is extended to the loyal subscribers of *Success Now! The Artrepreneur Newsletter for Fine Artists*, and *Manhattan Arts International*. I thank everyone who encouraged me to write this book and waited patiently for it to be completed. I am grateful to those who have purchased and recommended my previous books: *New York Contemporary Art Galleries: The Complete Annual Guide* and *Presentation Power Tools For Fine Artists*.

This book would not have come to fruition without the support of my immediate family – the source of my personal power. My mother Elyse's unwavering confidence in me has laid the foundation. My brother Pete's rock-solid discipline is a source of stability. My sister Selene's legacy of talent, courage and sacrifice will always inspire me to further my goals. My Aunt Sharon and Uncle Jay provide the stimuli for my spiritual growth. My father Zoltan's sensitivity, my aunt Gertie's generosity and love for humanity, and the pragmatic words of Gordon, my stepfather and mentor, continue to guide me on my journey.

But it is the next generation – my nephews, Michael and Jason, my nieces Cheri and Vanessa, and my cousins Jessica and Michael – who lovingly remind me each day that creativity is the perfect child within us. It is a precious gift that must be respected and nurtured, and allowed to blossom fully, because it is the essence of our souls and the path to our enlightenment.

Table of Contents

Acknowledgments — 4

Renée Phillips, The Author — 9

Introduction — 11
   Success *Now!* — 11
   Why I Wrote this Book — 13
   My Journey — 15

***Chapter 1:* It All Begins with You, The Artist** — 19
   Make Your Mark — 21
   Follow Your Passion — 22
   Dare to Dream — 25
   Don't Lock Yourself In — 27

***Chapter 2:* Myths, Fairy Tales &**
The Dangers of Self-Sabotage — 29
   "I'm an Artist, Not a Businessperson" — 32
   "The Poor, Starving Artist" — 35
   "The Sleeping Beauty Syndrome"
   Also known as "Someday My Prince(ss) will Come" — 37
   "All I Need is a (New York) Gallery" — 38

***Chapter 3:* The Truth about New York Galleries** — 41
   Getting Started — 43
   How to Approach — 45
   Use Protection — 50
   Paying to Show — 51
   Does it Ever Pay to Pay? — 55
   Questions to Ask Before Taking the Plunge — 56

Chapter 4: **5 Keys to Success** — **59**
- Confidence — 60
- Commitment — 62
- Persistence — 65
- Courage — 67
- Change — 68
- Powerful Questions that Lead to Change — 70

Chapter 5: **Relationships Create Your Power Base** — **71**
- The Art of Networking — 73
- Getting Psyched to Network — 76
- Camaraderie — 77
- The Power of Arts Organizations — 78
- Go! Go! Get a Coach! — 82

Chapter 6: **Where Have All the Women Gone?** — **85**
- Staggering Statistics — 85
- Perception of the Woman/Mother — 88
- A New Generation and Changes to Come — 89

Chapter 7: **Taking Care of Business: The Role of the Artrepreneur** — **91**
- The Rule of Thirds: Creator, Promoter and Administrator — 93
- A Success Story: The Artist who Applied "The Rule of Thirds" — 95
- Cash Flow — 97
- Time Management — 99
- 17 Time-Saving Tips — 100
- The Power of the Circle — 105

Chapter 8: **Create Your Master Plan! Master Your Destiny!** — **107**
- Your Career Goals — 110
- Your Financial Goals — 113
- Use "Green Power": Seize Your Potential for Wealth — 114

Visualize Your Goals	117
Enjoy the Process	118
Celebrate!	121
Your Career Goal: An Exercise	123
Your Financial Goal: An Exercise	124

Chapter 9: **Competitions: Are they Worth the Gamble?** — 125

A Toss of the Dice	126
Big-Name Jurors	127
Competitions as Fair Game	127
The Financial Picture	128
Artists Beware	129
Warning Signs	129
Proceed with Caution	130
How to be Competitive	130

Chapter 10: **Rejection: It's All a Matter of Perspective** — 133

Rejection as a Catalyst	133
The Importance of Objectivity	134
Dollars and Sense	135
Don't Burn Your Bridges	138
Luck is when Preparation Meets Opportunity	140
The "o" in No Stands for Opportunity	141

Chapter 11: **Taking Your Art to Market** — 143

Identifying Your Market	145
Your Customer Profile	147
Who and *Where* are the Buyers?	148
Building Your Mailing List	150
A Marketing Success Story	151
The Corporate Challenge	152
Feng Shui	155
Finding Markets through Art Fairs	156
Markets for Your Work are Everywhere: 80 Venues and Resources from A To Z	158

Chapter 12: **Successful Selling** — 159

Want to Increase Sales? You May Need to
Reject Some Myths — 160
Selling Your Art in an Exhibition — 165
Successful Selling Techniques — 167
After the Sale — 170
Understanding the Resistance to Buying Art — 171
Pricing Your Work — 173

Chapter 13: **The P's & Q's of Public Relations** — 175

Raise the Volume — 176
Different Ways to Shine — 178
Getting Your Fifteen Minutes — 179
Volunteer for P.R. Success — 183

Chapter 14: **The Art of Communication** — 187

The Power of Keeping a Journal — 191
Art Heals: From My Journal, July 30, 1996 — 192

Appendix 1: **80 Mantras for Success** — 195

Appendix 2: **Selected Artists' Groups, Arts Organizations, Councils and Foundations** — 197

Appendix 3: **Recommended Books** — 208

Appendix 4: **Recommended Periodicals** — 212

Index — 215

Upcoming Workshops — 222

Other Books by Renée Phillips — 225

Order Form — 229

Renée Phillips, The Author

Renée Phillips is the author of the First, Second and Third Editions of *New York Contemporary Art Galleries: The Complete Annual Guide*, hailed by the art community as the most comprehensive book of its kind, and *Presentation Power Tools For Fine Artists*. She is founder and Editor-in-Chief of *Manhattan Arts International* magazine which provides exposure to under-recognized artists. She is editor of *Success Now! For Artists: The Artrepreneur Newsletter For Fine Artists* and is a member of the International Art Critics' Association. Her articles have appeared in many publications including *The Artist's Proof*, a publication of New York Artists Equity Association, in which she held a position on the Board of Directors.

She has juried and curated more than 50 art exhibitions in alternative spaces and galleries, including Lincoln Center and National Arts Club. As an arts advocate she organized the *"Manhattan Arts* Debate," moderated by Tony Randall, which was the only political debate in the history of New York to concentrate solely on issues of the arts. It received widespread TV and print media coverage.

As a pioneer in her field, she has counseled and coached artists and agents world-wide. Her motivational seminars have been held at many universities and art institutions including Marymount Manhattan College, City College, Heckscher Museum, Katonah Museum, Columbia University, Bergen Museum, and for such organizations as the American Society of Contemporary Artists, NYC Teacher's College Association, New York Society of Women Artists, and Artists Talk on Art. She presents "Artists: How to Break into New York Galleries", which she created for The Learning Annex, and "Success Now!" workshops, in New York City.

For her contributions to the Arts she has been awarded citations from New York City's mayors Edward Koch and David Dinkins. She was featured in *New York Newsday* as a "Community Leader." She has been listed in the *World's Who Who of Women*, *Who's Who in American Art*, *The International Year Book and Statesmen's Who's Who* and *Community Leaders of the World*. Articles about her have appeared in *Crain's New York Business*, *The New York Times*, *Japan-New York*, and *Our Town*. She has appeared on many radio and TV programs.

As a professional artist, she sold her work to many private and corporate collectors, including Merrill Lynch, Chase Manhattan Bank, and Mr. and Mrs. Corwin, of Panasonic. She studied art at the American Art School, Art Students League, F.I.T. and School of Visual Arts.

*Success should not be measured
by external events –
when you sell your first work,
or have your first one-person show,
or get a positive review by a critic,
or when your work is collected by a museum.
It should be a constant flame that glows
steadily and triumphantly within you –
originating from the knowledge
that you create your destiny.
You don't need anyone –
a dealer, an agent, an art critic or patron –
to give you validation or approval.
Success – is yours – Now!*

Introduction

Success *Now!*

Follow your bliss.
Joseph Campbell

This book is a tribute to every artist who has the impulse to raise his or her voice and claim their identity – to break through the constraints that threaten their dignity and creative freedom. It champions the artist who passionately perseveres in a world that does not always nurture or appreciate the artist's contribution to the growth and healing of civilization. It is a companion for the artist who sometimes feels isolated during the process of producing and marketing their art.

For nearly two decades I have been blessed with having the opportunity to counsel thousands of artists and artists' agents from a wide range of ages, professional experience, education and ethnic backgrounds. They have sought my advice on countless career objectives and issues, from assembling their presentation documents and selecting a gallery to pricing and promoting their work. Much of the foundation for this book is derived from these experiences.

The title of this book is based on a monthly newsletter, *Success Now! For Artists*, which I started in 1991, to assist artists worldwide. It is also the title I have used in workshops over the years. I have had the privilege of bringing "Success Now!" seminars to audiences comprised of part- and full-time artists and educators in colleges, galleries, museums and arts organizations, such as the American Society of Contemporary Artists, New York Artist's Equity Association and NYC College Art Teachers Association. And, as a member of the faculty of Marymount Manhattan College, I presented a series of workshops titled "The Successful Artist in the New Millennium."

My friend and esteemed art writer Edward Rubin has succinctly referred to my writing as "a compendium of compassion, a labor of love." The essays in this book include topics I have discussed passionately in my seminars and private consultations, as well as articles I have written for *Manhattan Arts International* magazine, *Success Now! For Artists* newsletter, *The Artist's Proof* and other publications.

Throughout the book I discuss specific cases with clients and I have substituted different first names in order to retain their privacy. The book contains both inspirational and practical strategies and solutions in the areas of creating, marketing, selling and promotion.

The quotes sprinkled throughout the book originate from three primary sources, in addition to my own: *Artist to Artist*, compiled by Clint Brown; *An Artist's Book of Inspiration*, compiled and edited by Astrid Fitzgerald; and *And I Quote*, by Ashton Applewhite, William R. Evans III and Andrew Frothingham. The following quote from Deepak Chopra's book *The Seven Laws of Success* reflects much of the basis of this book:

You are what your deep, driving desire is.
As you desire it, so is your will.
As you will it, so is your deed.
As your deed is, so is your destiny.
Brihadaranyaka Upanishad IV. 4.5

You have to leave the city of your comfort
and go into the wilderness of your intuition.
What you'll discover will be wonderful.
What you'll discover will be yourself.
Alan Alda

Why I Wrote This Book

As I reflect on my professional journey over two decades I am aware of significant changes. When I began public speaking on art career topics in 1980, many artists objected to my insistence on their acquiring business skills. Now, most artists are eager to acquire knowledge and direction. Every day I receive dozens of calls from artists with an array of questions and each week I conduct workshops on the business of being an artist.

I listen attentively to what artists say they want and don't want, especially the deeper issues – the artists' attitudes, needs, beliefs – the kind of persons they are and want to be for "success" and "happiness" on their own terms. We frequently discuss what is happening on a more profound level – what roadblocks may be deterring them from attaining their objectives. We focus on solving problems and nourishing the power they have within as well as obtaining outside resources that are available to assist them.

There are many career challenges that await artists at different stages of their development. I've learned no matter how many opportunities and leads are provided, they will not help an artist who flounders because he or she lacks long-term goals and strategies and the proper guidance and perseverance to bring them to fruition. The aim of this book is to help artists to examine the tough issues that may impede their growth and increase their vulnerability, such as making aimless career decisions, self-sabotage, and dependency. It asks many questions as well as offers answers in these areas. Practical topics are also addressed, such as those concerning cash flow, time-management, networking, marketing, selling, promotion and publicity.

Success Now! For Artists is an invitation to discover and develop your innate strengths and powers, to clarify your goals, take charge of your careers and pursue your dreams in a place of serenity and celebration. I hope it stimulates and supports you along every step of your professional journey. In the back of the book you will find "80 Mantras for Success" – a place you can go to quickly recharge your batteries.

> *Life is either a daring adventure or nothing.*
> Helen Keller

I believe that one teaches most fervently those things that one needs to learn. The impetus behind every word that I write and speak is my need to share, to learn and to grow with you.

Although the process of writing this book began in 1991, the true meaning of *Success Now!* has become more urgent to me in the last two years, my having faced two personal tragedies. One was the sudden death of my sister, a loving, beautiful and talented woman whose life came to an abrupt end before she could achieve her creative potential. Since her death, my relationship with my two nephews has fueled my life with a poignant sense of responsibility – to encourage them to fulfill their dreams and live rewarding and productive lives. And, within the last two years, my mother was diagnosed with Alzheimer's Disease. As her primary caretaker, I am faced daily with new challenges to cope with this debilitating disease. I am tested on my capacity for compassion, patience and communication.

Most importantly, these painful experiences have shown me how to cherish every precious moment that brings opportunities to discover, love and learn. They have encouraged me to be more persistent and passionate about reaching out to artists – to guide them on their path to self-discovery and well-being.

The insightful words of Henry Miller offer reassurance and direction:

> *Everything we shut our eyes to,*
> *everything we run away from,*
> *everything we deny, denigrate or despise,*
> *serves to defeat us in the end.*
> *What seems nasty, painful, evil, can become a source*
> *of beauty, joy, and strength, if faced with an open mind.*
> *Every moment is a golden one for him*
> *who has the vision to recognize it as such.*

My Journey

When I was a full time artist, I refused to accept the notion of being anything *but* an artist. I rebelled against anything that threatened to steal artistic freedom from me. I indulged daily in a playground of creative ecstasy, and was equally rewarded in the process of selling my art work and receiving recognition. While I watched other artists struggle to find the same freedom of choice, I was propelled to get out from behind my easel and organize and promote group exhibitions, share resources, write, and counsel artists about the business of art.

On the journey to fulfill our purpose in life, from the very beginning, we learn from both positive and negative events that shape our destiny. As a child, several years of ballet lessons taught me discipline and endurance. As an active student council representative in high school, I advocated students' rights, and as a cheerleader, I coached my team mates onto victory. As the daughter of an alcoholic and abusive father, I developed survival skills and self-esteem. At age ten, I began to devour psychology books, trying to understand the complexities of human behavior. My desire to assist the disempowered was kindled and I yearned to pursue a career in counseling and public service with aspirations to join the Peace Corps. While in college, as a volunteer at Suffolk Psychiatric Hospital, I discovered the limitations of bureaucratic "rehabilitation." I continued my search for my professional identity outside the system and found fulfillment in creating and teaching art. The love and respect I developed for art and artists inspired me to embark on my career journey which led me to exactly where I am, and where I am supposed to be *Now!*

A major turning point in my life occurred in 1980 when I left the suburbs of Long Island and moved to Manhattan. The City's creative vitality and diverse cultural communities exhilarated me – and still do. I also quickly learned that most artists feel powerless to penetrate the formidable ivory tower that is known as the art business community. With the encouragement of a group of artist friends, and inspired by Thomas More's *Utopia*, I forged ahead and formed *Artopia*, a multi-media arts organization. In that capacity, I organized multi-media art exhibitions in a wide variety of alternative spaces and galleries – from Wall Street to Lincoln Center. I joined New York Artists Equity, a vital artists advocacy organization, where I was elected to the Board of Directors. My writing articles for art publications and newspapers led to the creation of *Fusion-Arts Review* in 1983, which was renamed *Manhattan Arts International* in 1985. It is devoted to promoting the work of under-recognized artists as well as providing valuable information about art professionals and institutions. These formative years confirmed my belief that I could find a place in which to make a meaningful contribution.

For nearly twenty years, I have led a rewarding career as a self-supporting *artrepreneur*. The work I am doing *now* – writing, counseling and public speaking – is exactly what I want to be doing *now*. I am extremely blessed to have a career that supports me, and yet I never "go to work." Every day my time is mine to dream, discover, dialogue, create, learn, teach, write, coach and advise. Every project I pursue is in response to filling the professional artist's needs, and I am richly rewarded with personal growth. The individuals I serve are not merely my clients, they are my extended family.

There are so many creative, intelligent individuals putting their dreams on hold. The concept of waiting until "someday" to begin living a rewarding life, has always struck me as sad and unacceptable. My concept of success was deftly expressed by Bob Dylan who wrote:

A man is a success
if he gets up in the morning
and goes to bed at night
and in between does what he wants to do.

I love making art...
It's largely how I see myself.
I'm an artist,
therefore I have to make art.
Chuck Close

Chapter 1

It All Begins With You: The Artist

*If art is to nourish the roots of our culture,
society must set the artist free
to follow his vision wherever it takes him...
We must never forget that art is not a form
of propaganda; it is a form of truth.*
John F. Kennedy

The contemporary art world is a complex and fascinating web of art and commerce. It depends upon a diverse number of individuals, each one contributing in some way by playing a crucial role, none more noticeably important than the other – except for the artist.

The artist's influence on the world of real estate is staggering. Groups of determined artists have been responsible for transforming bleak districts into desirable, posh enclaves, such as SoHo, Tribeca and Chelsea, in New York City, as well as

Provincetown, the Hamptons and London's Chelsea, to name a few. However, rather than being supported and revered for their efforts toward renovating, gentrifying and beautifying their environment, their rewards are unjust rent hikes and eviction.

If there were no artists, millions of art dealers, framers, supply manufacturers, photographers, critics, auctioneers, museum curators and publishers, would have to seek other professions. If it were not for the artist and their creativity, our civilization would suffer from stagnation, despair and chaos. Without art, we would become dehumanized.

Remember, it all begins with you. As an artist you are especially endowed with success. Each day is an opportunity to celebrate the gifts that have been bestowed upon you. You have an acute sensitivity to a myriad of stimuli. You have the power to create something that, before you imagined it, did not exist. With a blank canvas or sheet of paper, a slab of clay, hunk of stone, camera lens, found objects or computer technology, you are capable of bringing inner visions to outer forms by expressing your strongest urges. You possess a unique power to elicit a response, alter a person's consciousness and have a major impact on those who see your work, as well as being able to change the course of art history!

It is cause for celebration! You owe it to yourself and to others with every breath you take to use your innate capacities to their greatest extent; to claim your voice and to tell your story, to share your gifts and to enrich and deepen our understanding of the human condition.

Art is the opposite of nature.
A work of art can come only from the interior of man.
Edvard Munch

> *I paint my own reality.*
> *I paint because I need to, and I paint always*
> *whatever passes through my head,*
> *without any other consideration.*
> Frida Kahlo

Make Your Mark

The artist is born with a compelling need to probe the depths of self-expression and proclaim self-liberation. The challenge that lies before them is no small task – to explore their innate creativity, fight the demons, ignore the critical internal voices, discover their strengths and push them to the maximum, and firmly place their inimitable handprint on the Earth with conviction. With no regrets!

When I am asked to examine an artist's portfolio or write an article, I look for that handprint – the signs that reveal how well the artist has found his or her own voice and has shaped feelings and ideas into unique forms. I always hope to find that spark of genius, that *extraordinary* mark of innovation that always makes my heart beat faster.

Art that is noticeably "derivative" of another artist's style and reflects very little of the artist's personal view of the world shows that the artist is prevented from asserting his or her own identity. Chuck Close, a major artist of this century, expressed it well when he said that he felt "trapped" in other artists' painting styles, as an abstract expressionist, until he formulated "new ways to make marks that make art." All artists must first master their craft and then transcend it – forget everything that others taught them and place their craft on automatic pilot. Eventually, they must let go of their crutches and fly solo. And, when they soar they lift the world with them.

*I decided I was a very stupid fool
not to at least paint as I wanted to
and say what I wanted to when I painted,
as that seemed to be the only thing I could do
that didn't concern anybody but myself.*
Georgia O'Keefe

Follow Your Passion

Artists ask me: Which style should I pursue? Where is the market going? They anxiously jump from one body of work to another as if they were chasing the elusive rainbow. I tell them to be present in the moment – to be committed to creating the best work they possibly can and, only then, will the path to the right market place become apparent to them.

If you are not totally committed to your art, you will fail yourself and your audience. All the marketing strategies, exhibitions and sales will not compensate for the lack of sincerity and motivation.

Bob was plagued with indecision when he approached me for direction. He was represented by a few galleries in the United States. He asked me to help him find a New York gallery and develop marketing strategies. During the consultation, he expressed his pleasure in having steady sales, but he felt dissatisfied with the direction of his work. His paintings were attractive, colorful abstracts, but they lacked the spark of vitality and spontaneity. The work, I learned, was largely influenced by his dealer's demands to fill a certain niche in the gallery. If Bob changed direction he could possibly face the loss of income and representation.

I encouraged Bob to discuss the subjects that stimulated him. He began to speak passionately about his love for animals and his disgust of our government's indifference toward endangered species. In his spare time he served as a volunteer for an animal protection organization.

We discussed his apprehension about giving up the security he now had and his desire to create art that was more gratifying to him. I explained that he was entitled to have both and did not have to choose between the two.

After the initial consultation, Bob began a new series of work. He experienced a creative breakthrough and completed several paintings in a few months.

Shortly, thereafter, we launched a vigorous marketing and publicity campaign. We arranged a few exhibitions, and I introduced him to a product licenser who developed new marketing areas for him. Our media campaign resulted in local and national press attention. The gallery that sold his abstract paintings was more than happy to represent his new work.

Bob is now a successful wildlife painter aligned with leading environmental and animal rights organizations. His art celebrates the majestic beauty of endangered species and it reflects the importance of healing the Earth. Some of his images have been reproduced in limited edition serigraphs and note cards with national distribution.

He is proud that he accomplished his goal as a creative person – an artist with a mission who has helped to raise the consciousness of millions of people. He approaches his work with enthusiasm because his paintings are honest and unedited expressions of his convictions.

The minute I sat in front of a canvas, I was happy.
Because it was a world, and I could do as I like in it.
Alice Neel

When you find the sources of inspiration and stimulation, and release yourself to them, the art will create itself. Make a habit of noticing the things that really excite you – the subjects and events that stir you to the core of your being – and follow those intense feelings.

You must create art first, then look for the appropriate market and venue. You will be deceiving yourself if you reverse the order, or if you conform to market and dealers' demands.

Your art is a reflection of how you respond to life – your emotions, your experiences, your values, beliefs and choices – the sum of what makes you unique. Let it shine. Let it resonate. Let it rejoice. Let it echo and reverberate throughout the world. Let it shock. Let it rock. Let it console. Let it cajole. Let it explode. Let it break all the rules. Let it claim new frontiers. Release it. Let it flood the universe. Let it run amuck. Let it make a ruckus. Let it fill the air with song. Let it be.

Here I am...happy, completely happy.
I have had a wonderful day of painting.
It is not that I have accomplished
anything in particular,
but it's the thought of all I could do
that makes me almost crazy with joy.
Paula Modersohn-Becker

> *To become truly immortal*
> *a work of art must escape all human limits:*
> *logic and common sense will only interfere.*
> *But once these barriers are broken it will enter*
> *the regions of childhood vision and dream.*
>
> Giorgio De Chirico

Dare to Dream

Barbara brought her portfolio to me and, it contained over fifty slides and represented five years of her figurative paintings. Her work reflected discipline and superb technical skills.

She showed me three different series, two of which were quite prosaic, and one was extraordinary. I was awe-struck by a provocative, half human/half animal form that spontaneously leapt from the paintings. I asked her where this beautifully odd creature came from. Her embarrassment revealed that I had entered a very private realm. After some hesitation, her trust in me grew, and she invited me in. She told me her imagery originated from her dreams. She explained that she had produced many drawings of it, but cast them aside as silly doodles. The voice in her head seemed to utter rejection and humiliation: "These paintings are strange and people will think you are crazy. No one will like them. No one will buy them."

We continued to discuss the compelling images that attracted me for their refreshing honesty, but disturbed her. I encouraged her to release the wonderful mysteries and messages that appeared in her dreams. As we discussed the intriguing possibility of letting this creature evolve, I realized that I had given her permission to identify and accept the beautiful child in her that had been thwarted by judgment and ridicule.

Since our first meeting, Barbara has translated more of her dream images into her paintings, and she is producing a magnificent and prolific body of work. The positive responses she is receiving, including juried exhibitions and awards, have erased her feelings of self-consciousness. She has discovered the joyful process of creative freedom, and she is empowered by a clarity of vision.

By exploring the unknown and having the courage to risk derision, Barbara also developed more confidence in other areas of her life. She befriended a group of artists whose work is also profound and daring. With them she has participated in several successful exhibitions. She broke through the barriers that prevented her from capturing a wider audience and recognition.

There are many discoveries about yourself waiting to be revealed. Begin uncovering them by investigating your dreams. You never know what you may find in the treasure chest of your individuality, beliefs and passions.

I'll take weeks out doing drawings,
watercolor studies, I may never use.
I'll throw them in a backroom, never look at them again
or drop them on the floor and walk over them.
But I feel that the communion that
has seeped into the subconscious
will eventually come out in the final picture.
Andrew Wyeth

*It is imagination
that gives depth and space to a picture.*
Henri Matisse

Don't Lock Yourself In

Cohesion is an important attribute when bringing your art to the public arena. Dealers look for an aesthetic similitude – something they can key into when they publicize and sell your work. Many artists are aware of having continuity in their work, especially when they produce a series. A fully articulated, consistent idea, however, must not be confused with redundant, cookie-cutter production. Be careful not to "brand" yourself with a single expression that is too restrictive, or to rush prematurely into the spotlight with your first group of works. Give yourself and your work the chance to develop and reflect a creative range.

A few years ago after seeing some of Simon's work we invited him to be featured in the magazine. He showed me his latest series of paintings which he created in the last two years. In addition to asking me to select the images for the publication he asked for advice in choosing the pieces to go into his upcoming one-person exhibition. Simon's work focused on human suffering. His palette, predominately greens and blues, heightened an overall sense of malaise. He had developed a distinctive style and poignant approach to his subject matter.

Curious to see how he had evolved, I asked Simon to show me his earlier works. Although the styles were definitely the same, his previous paintings represented a broader range of expressions and colors. He was clearly an artist who had achieved a heightened maturity. Every painting conveyed the soul of his subjects.

In our discussions, Simon said that although his new works were melancholy, he had no desire to proclaim himself as an artist portraying angst and suffering, but rather, to encompass the vast well-spring of humanity. And, indeed, his versatile compositions reflected that kind of energy, reinforcing the heart-felt motivation behind his work.

We decided to incorporate Simon's earlier works into the exhibition and the magazine. If we had featured only his recent paintings, we would have limited his audience's interpretation of his work. Instead, with diversity we increased his audience and enhanced the interest in his work. The exposure encouraged him to continue to stretch his vocabulary.

*Generally speaking,
color directly influences the soul.
Color is the keyboard, the eyes are the hammers,
the soul is the piano with many strings.
The artist is the hand that plays,
touching one key or another purposively,
to cause vibrations in the soul.*
Vasilly Kandinsky

Chapter 2

Myths, Fairy Tales and The Dangers of Self-Sabotage

*If you could kick the person
responsible for most of your troubles,
you would not be able to sit down for months.*
Unknown

In addition to creating the art, the artist who wants to earn a living is required to navigate through a complex terrain of administrative tasks, marketing strategies, negotiations and technical applications. Unfortunately, in today's world, many talented artists flounder because they fail to develop even the smallest amount of business acumen.

If we were to look for a reason why artists are besieged by sorrow, we wouldn't have to look very far. Some of the common causes are: the insensitive parent that discourages them from pursuing dreams, the government and general society that often ignores the significance of the arts, and the traditional educational system that fails to prepare the artist for the harsh realities of the professional art world – to name a few.

For centuries artists have had to endure many obstacles, and in recent years since art has become big business, it is often difficult to circumvent them and find the doorways to opportunities. Many artists who are unprepared to function effectively in the business of art become enraged and cynical toward this imperfect, unfair system of competition, demands, controls and power struggles. They resent having to be subservient to the individuals they have to depend on for support. Their defense is either to lash out at the commercial establishment or withdraw into a fantasy world where they wait hopefully for something or someone to magically rescue them. Both are disabling states of inertia that stifle the artist's creative urges and make it impossible to find an audience.

> *As long as a man*
> *stands in his own way,*
> *everything seems to be in his way.*
> Ralph Waldo Emerson

Many artists waste tremendous energy waging war on too many trivial fronts and pursuing lost causes. When faced with a possible adversary remember you never know who you may need – who might someday be in a position to advance your career or sabotage it. We all make enemies along the way, but it is important to focus on attracting more allies.

We need to stop agonizing over what *cannot* be changed in the outside reality and look within for direction. Sometimes self-sabotage may be the larger obstacle.

There are several ways that artists can sabotage themselves: by being overly sensitive to criticism, by refusing to take the responsibility for their careers, and by continually clinging to bitterness. Self-sabotage occurs when artists lie on their resumes or show blatant disrespect toward someone who could help them. They sabotage their careers when they submit poor quality slides to a jury, or when they wait until the last minute to mail their show invitations, or when they fail to follow up on a lead for a sale. They are their own worst enemies when they enter a relationship with an abusive dealer and allow themselves to be subservient, but somehow feel they have no choice.

As difficult as it may seem, there are ways for artists to survive and thrive in the maze of business. The first step is to develop and sustain a realistic and positive outlook. Artists must also stand firm and confident. Personal journals, meditation, one-on-one spiritual or psychological therapy, support groups, traveling, visiting museums, and exploring new media can offer encouragement and inspiration. Artists must also accept responsibility for their successes and failures, and they must empower themselves with knowledge, camaraderie and business skills.

The path to empowerment begins by rejecting the negative voices that creep into the dark corners of your mind. Myths have pervaded artists' lives for centuries. These myths have perpetuated the notion that the artists are subservient to dealers, collectors and critics. The careers of many artists have been harmed because the artists have accepted these myths as facts. This has resulted in stereotypes: "I'm An Artist, Not A Business Person", "The Poor Starving Artist", "The Sleeping Beauty Syndrome (also known as "Someday My Prince(ss) Will Come)" and "All I Need Is A (New York) Gallery."

> *Every human being on this earth*
> *is born with a tragedy, and it isn't original sin.*
> *He's born with the tragedy that he has to grow up.*
> *A lot of people don't have the courage to do it.*
> Helen Hayes

"I'm an Artist, Not a Businessperson"

"I can't handle business", artists will tell me, as if it were a dreadful disease that will contaminate their artistic abilities. The very thought of it makes their blood boil and their creative juices freeze.

The fact that most artists today are unprepared for the professional art world is not entirely their fault. For centuries, they have been told that they lack business sophistication. It is only recently that art business courses have been offered to artists to assist them, although these limited courses are not required. Unfortunately, artists graduate with a misguided fantasy that someone else will be responsible for preparing promotional documents, dealing with the press, marketing and selling their art, along with contacting galleries, museums and art consultants, and fulfilling the other obligations to further their careers. When they learn the truth the hard way it shocks them and, without survival skills, their hopes dissipate quickly. They believe the only avenue open to them is to wait on tables or to get into the commercial field, or somewhere in between.

Taking care of business does not mean you have to sacrifice the integrity of your work. And, being an artist does not automatically disable you from comprehending basic business principles. In fact, the best entrepreneurs – in any field – are those individuals who exercise a creative approach to problem-solving.

It takes time and patience to develop new skills. When you were born, you were not able to could walk or talk, but, eventually, you learned to master these abilities. What an amazing transformation you made in a very short period of time! As an artist pursuing a successful business career, you may have to crawl at first, and you may have to perform many tedious tasks, often stumbling, before you can walk and excel.

> *One can never consent to creep*
> *when one feels an impulse to soar.*
> Helen Keller

Early in my own artistic career, business was my enemy. However, I soon realized that it was a means to an end: creative freedom. One of my freelance jobs was to paint on fabric for an established fashion designer in the Hamptons. She laid bolts of silks and cottons on a table, and I painted anything I desired – mostly natural motifs. One day, I did an entire wedding party ensemble – from hats to shoes! I was forced to work in a hot, tiny, crowded room in the back of a posh boutique, so I focused my thoughts on the joyful process of painting, and I imagined how the people would look dressed in wearable art.

After my work was completed, the designer signed her name to the garments. Her affluent customers paid a high price for "her" hand-painted apparel. She received the glory for my creative efforts, while I received money that went to pay the rent for my studio, where I could paint my own canvases and sign my own name. The compensation was fair and I accepted the experience as a short-term sacrifice for reaching a long-term goal.

It was in this designer's boutique that I learned my first business lessons that helped me to strive toward becoming self-sufficient. I learned about the importance of using money as a tool. I learned that if I wanted to earn more money from my creative work, I would have to find a way to gain a reputation of my own. That's when I made a commitment to obtain knowledge in the areas of self-promotion and publicity. My disdain for having to work for someone else, and the need to be my own boss, were the stimuli I needed to succeed.

Today, I know of many artists who are earning a living in the arts and creating their fine art without having to compromise their goals. To augment the sales earned from their art, they channel their talents in many directions – from accepting graphic art assignments, to designing websites, to teaching and to giving art museum tours.

Very few people know how to work.
Inspiration, everybody has inspiration, that's just hot air.
Beatrice Wood

On the road to self-sufficiency, we have many teachers. Some reveal themselves in the historical biographies of Matisse, Rubens, Picasso, and Dali, as well as books by Napoleon Hill, Norman Vincent Peale, and Dale Carnegie. Self-help and inspirational books, workshops and living role models are everywhere. You should adapt the techniques and life style that suit your values and personality. Leave your innocence where it produces the best results – in your art – and learn to adopt some pragmatic rules to become proficient in the real world.

Everything you need you already have.
You are complete right now, you are a whole,
total person, not an apprentice person
on the way to someplace else.
Your completeness must be understood by you
and experienced in your thoughts
as your own personal reality.
Wayne Dyer

"The Poor, Starving Artist"

It is time to bury this myth! For decades, it has served to create an aura of romance and mystique which helps to market books and art work by artists who have more value to art sellers through their posthumous reputations. The negative stereotype of the pathetic, neurotic artist living in an unkempt garret, eating sardines and stale bread, and drinking cheap wine, victimizes all living artists. It robs them of their power to prosper with dignity. Rather than hearing about Vincent van Gogh's malaise and the countless theories on why he cut his ear, or about artists who have died from AIDS and overdosed on drugs, I prefer to read and discuss success stories about artists who have triumphed over challenges. "The Poor, Starving Artist" needs to be replaced with "The Self-Empowered Artist."

There are times when you may think that you must be crazy to have chosen this profession. Members of your family may proclaim that you are naïve and immature, and ask you, "When will you give up your obsession and pursue a *real* career? Why can't you be more like your cousin Michael the accountant or your sister Anne the lawyer?" Hopefully, you have learned to ignore these questions and find the courage to be a non-conformist. Follow your creative path with confidence and determination, and you will grow stronger with every step of the process.

The term, "The Poor, Starving Artist," is an oxymoron. While others may define their wealth and their success by how many material objects they can possess, the artist is richly rewarded with self-fulfillment and by creating something with his or her own imagination and hands. Many individuals outside the art profession feel dehumanized, like cogs in the machinery of capitalism – highly-paid, perhaps, but highly-stressed – starving for identity and job satisfaction. Striving for money, fame, popularity and position without a spiritual foundation, leaves them searching for the deeper meaning of life. The rapid expansion of the Self-Improvement section of bookstores in recent years reflects this epidemic.

There is only one success –
to be able to spend your life in your own way.
Christopher Morley

The emphasis should not be placed on the paycheck you receive after a week of dreary toil, but the measure of fulfillment in every moment you spend in the process of creating your work. Money and job security fluctuate. Possessions can be lost in a flood or fire. They are not permanent, nor do they represent the innate talent and resources you possess.

Many artists may choose to hide behind the stereotype of "The Poor, Starving Artist." This is to avoid responsibility and mature behavior. They often find themselves victimized by those who enjoy exercising their power. Sadly, the artist who accepts this self-fulfilling prophecy will never know the rich rewards of self-empowerment and self-employment. There is an increasing number of artists who have shattered this myth and forged a path to prosperity and independence. An artist who needs reassurance or guidance may find it beneficial to seek out positive role models and emulate them.

*Some people dream of success,
while others wake up and work hard to attain it.*

"The Sleeping Beauty Syndrome"
Also known as
"Someday My Prince(ss) Will Come"

Wouldn't it be nice to hear the proverbial tap on your studio door from the magnanimous patron or benevolent art dealer, who recognizes your artistic abilities and leads you to eternal bliss? Envision your benefactors and admirers as they tiptoe toward your door and slip large amounts of cash and rave reviews under it, then walk quietly away, leaving you undisturbed, in peace, to spend the rest of your life creating art.

Illusion is much more appealing than reality, but it is pragmatism that builds personal power. You know the lyrics: "Fairy tales can come true, they can happen to you…" But let me add: "…if you're willing to commit yourself to hard work." Artists are "discovered" after they have accumulated merit and achieved their rightful place by proving to have artistic and investment value through exhibitions, competitions, awards and sales.

If you choose to believe in fantasies you will become disillusioned and end up feeling like a failure, ineffective and dependent on others. Instead of waiting passively for that magical moment to arrive when checks and rave reviews roll in, take action. Hire the best representative you can – yourself. Plan an active career, continue to develop self-sufficiency and, only then will you attract the support from others. Be realistic, and you will feel powerful and capable.

> *The consuming desire of most human beings*
> *is deliberately to plant their whole life*
> *in the hands of some other person.*
> *I would describe this method*
> *of searching for happiness as immature.*
> *Development of character consists solely*
> *in moving toward self-sufficiency.*
> Quentin Crisp

"All I Need is a (New York) Gallery"

Many artists approach me from every corner of the globe to help them find a New York gallery and, on many occasions, I've been a good matchmaker.

For several years, my monthly workshop, "Artists: How to Break Into New York Galleries", has been filled with artists who have come for the key that will open the gallery door. Artists have flown here from all over the world to take my course. I don't have a magic pill to dispense or a magic wand to wave. What I offer is factual, useable information, and I strive to make sure that every artist leaves armed with the proper knowledge, focus and fortitude to approach galleries.

An artist's desire to seek entry to the best galleries in New York – the art capital of the world – is easily understood. There is great value in having solid representation by a reputable New York dealer. But, too often, artists focus only on this goal, many times prematurely, and they ignore the larger picture. They also fail to see the logistics of the equation – from the dealer's perspective.

An age old problem between artists and gallery owners is caused by a lack of understanding. Artists usually don't comprehend the challenges of operating a gallery, and dealers generally lack compassion for the artist. When an unknown artist who has sold only a few pieces, approaches a gallery for an exhibition, he or she may not take into consideration the gallery's overhead and the high level of risk the gallery owner must take. On the other hand, the dealer who has been inundated by packages from a wide variety of artists on a weekly basis (many of which are inappropriate for the direction of the gallery), may respond with a cold shoulder or a rejection form letter.

For an artist to succeed, the gallery must invest a vast amount of time and money toward promoting and marketing the artist's work. This commitment is generated by not only the art, but the artwork's marketing potential. Whether the artist is new or established, a gallery's commitment rarely comes with the guarantee that the art will sell. And, a contractual agreement does not always mean that the gallery will pay the artist in a timely fashion. It is possible that the gallery may go bankrupt, or it may decide to change its marketing direction, and that change may not include the artist.

One of the greatest misconceptions artists have is that once they belong to a gallery, all they have to do is create art. In truth, the gallery may expect much more. Part of your gallery relationship is to insure an *active, long-term* relationship. It is naïve to assume that after you deliver the work to the gallery your work is done. Successful artists follow up and follow through. They communicate routinely with their dealers and discuss career strategies that will enhance their sales and publicity.

*The gallery interviews
up to 50 artist applicants in person
and receives about 20 parcels
of slides and photos in the mail each week,
and visits the studios of those it considers
to have works worthy of close inspection.*
Ivan Karp, O.K. Harris Gallery

Chapter 3

The Truth About New York Galleries

Artists should have a credible representative body of work before they submit their slides... They should possess originality, a point of view, command of technique and commitment.
Heller Gallery

To thrive in this part of the world, you cannot be an insecure, vulnerable or naïve dilettante who lacks seriousness, ambition, courage, artistic talent and business acumen. In many ways, it is the survival of the fittest. But, after all this *is* New York!

There are more than 760 galleries and alternative exhibition spaces in New York City, and many of them are accessible to under-recognized artists. The terrain is vast and versatile, as well as complex and sometimes overwhelming – not only to outsiders, but to the artists who live right in the midst of its ever-changing scenery.

To assist artists in their search for appropriate galleries, every year, since 1995, I have produced and updated a comprehensive resource book titled *New York Contemporary Art Galleries: The Complete Annual Guide*. The galleries do not pay me to be included, and that makes it an honest and comprehensive survey. I also contact each owner and director directly to obtain the information first hand.

I collect the data from a questionnaire with 40 questions. Each listing includes contact names, owner's background, year established, hours of operation, gallery size, styles, media, prices, purpose or philosophy, number and origins of artists represented, the ratio of male and female artists, a selection of artists and a description of their work, the number of annual solo and group exhibitions, the publications in which the galleries advertise, their procedures for selecting artists, how and when artists, curators and organizations should approach the gallery, their requirements from artists, exhibition fees, membership dues, and artists' stipends.

The detailed information provided in this book has been referred to as "the bible of the industry" and "manna from heaven." It does everything short of reaching out and placing the artist in the right gallery, and it certainly makes the navigation less risky and time-consuming.

What I have learned from interviewing several hundred gallery owners each year is that we cannot stereotype dealers. There are as many different tastes, personalities and educational and cultural backgrounds as there are styles of art to be shown. Contrary to rumor, every gallery in New York does not show funky, avant-garde, cutting edge work; traditional styles are quite prevalent. And, not all of the New York dealers are unscrupulous; I have found most dealers to be very devoted to the art and the artists they represent, and hard working professionals who are trying to do their best in a difficult profession.

If you are thinking of approaching New York dealers, it's best to dismiss any pre-conceived notions, brush off any chip you may have on your shoulder and, above all, be persistent.

We look at new artists' slides almost every Thursday. Generally artists deliver slides in the AM and pick up after 3:00....
Nancy Hoffman

Getting Started

Many artists, who have illusions of achieving easy access to the highest tier of the gallery system, learn it is a process that requires a methodical, persistent and serious approach, and it takes effort and time to develop – beginning with the lower and middle rungs of the ladder. This is especially disconcerting to the artist from abroad who has established what they perceive as a successful career in their homebase. I advise most out of state artists to build reputations regionally before approaching New York galleries. Develop a strong exhibition history. Exhaust the best venues in your area.

Statistics prove that only a small number of artists have the kind of dealers and arrangements that can sustain their reputations and finances for many years. The cold, hard reality is that there are hundreds of thousands of artists who are all competing for the same galleries. Dan Concholar, Director of the Art Information Center in New York, has stated, that it takes at least seven years to penetrate the New York gallery system.

Many young artists who are new to this city in search for a gallery are often inexperienced and their art is undeveloped. They may lack the maturity that is required to make a commitment. It takes time to develop patience, education, experience and confidence. Without these virtues, the young artist is likely to make the wrong choices, which may be very painful ones. Often, the price the artist pays is the loss of independence or a strong dose of rejection.

Role: To focus on the development of contemporary art through its presentation – art that is often under-represented in larger museum and commercial gallery structures.
Art in General

For the artist who is ready and willing, New York offers a range of opportunities – from newly opened, privately owned galleries that are in the process of developing their core group of artists, to leading New York galleries that take on new artists. There are also several good cooperative galleries in which artist members share expenses and pay very low commissions on sales, or none at all.

There are ways to obtain exhibitions – almost immediately. In the beginning, to establish recognition and build collectors, take advantage of the plethora of alternative exhibition spaces and the non-profit venues that are mission-driven, not sales-driven. New York's universities and government-funded art institutions offer opportunities to obtain exposure, critical acclaim, and awards. Exhibition venues are possible by joining artist organizations that exhibit their members' work or entering their non-member juried competitions. Some of the organizations are national, while others are New York-based. Among them are: The National Sculpture Society, The Pastel Society, The Salmagundi Club, The American Watercolor Society, Burr Artists, Catharine Lorillard Wolfe Art Club, The Westside Arts Coalition, American Society of Contemporary Artists, National Association of Women Artists, New York Society of Women Artists, and others. *(See Appendix 2.)* Many public spaces welcome such artists' groups, such as Cork Gallery in Lincoln Center and Lever House on Park Avenue. And, don't ignore New York's synagogues, banks, libraries, book stores, corporate spaces, restaurants and cafés that offer opportunities to exhibit your work.

The best time for artists to submit materials is between January and February, and June and July. The artist must first familiarize themselves with the work the gallery represents.
Gallery Henoch

How to Approach

You probably know by now that the selection of art is subjective and, personal taste, personality and background, among others things, play a role. Some dealers allow the art to seduce them. They may use phrases like "falling in love with the art." Others concentrate on the bottom line, and look for commercial value.

Most dealers prefer that artists become familiar with the shows they mount and the aesthetic direction they pursue before submitting materials for consideration. Some dealers say that they do not want to be influenced by the artist and they prefer that the materials are sent in the mail, while other dealers have an open viewing policy and invite artists to call for an appointment.

The first step to finding an appropriate gallery is research. Locate leads through various art publications, such as *Manhattan Arts International, New York Contemporary Art Galleries, ARTnews, Art in America, Gallery Guide, Art in America's Guide to Museums, Galleries,* and *Artforum.* It is advisable to visit the galleries you have selected. If you cannot travel, try to make reliable contacts with other artists and art professionals in New York.

On your visits examine the lighting, gallery size, attitude of the personnel and the way the art is presented. Collect brochures and other documentation about the artists in the galleries that interest you. Keep abreast of the galleries' exhibitions and styles of art shown over several months, through reviews, advertisements and announcement cards. Inquire about the gallery's reviewing process and level of interest in new artists. Visit frequently in order to detect inconsistencies and changes. Attend their opening receptions and introduce yourself to the artists.

Take tips from resumes. The next time you visit a gallery that shows work that is similar to yours, ask to see the artist's catalogue or artist's book which is usually available to guests at the reception desk. It will serve as a sense of professional comparison. It will also offer leads to other exhibitions and collections of the artist. You can approach those leads with confidence that they accept similar work.

> *The gallery reviews new artists' materials in April.*
> *Artists should mail slides or photos, resume and SASE.*
> *Art must show a unique vision, art with poetry and spirituality,*
> *by artists who express their own vocabulary.*
> June Kelly

Your gallery presentation materials should include your cover letter, resume, slides and other visual documentation. They should be neatly organized in a pocket folder or binder. They should clearly explain the size and subject of your work and medium. The resume should call attention to exhibitions, awards, testimonials, collections, reviews, art-related experience, and other achievements that enhance the value of your art. They should adhere to excellent quality standards.

Most of the galleries request a slide sheet, although you will want to include larger visual reproductions of your work, especially if you are sending them for the first time without a referral. Remember, your purpose is to introduce them to your work in a format that is noticed, such as an impressive color catalogue. Also, 4" x 5" or 8" x 10" color transparencies, color photographs, color Xerox or digital prints, and CD-Roms and videos are being used by artists.

If you obtain an appointment with the gallery, do some homework. Before you meet find out as much as you can about the gallery and its owners in order to engage in a substantive dialogue. When meeting a dealer for the first time in their gallery, you should be able to converse intelligently about the current show, the direction of the gallery, and art history. Your conversation alone may not result in an exhibition, but your sincerity, homework and education will be noticed. Above all, it will place you on an equal professional level.

"A consistency of style and purpose" is a phrase that a dealer may use to describe maturity in an artist's development. You shouldn't confuse being "consistent" with boring repetition. The consistency a dealer refers to is a cohesive body of work which reflects the artist's unique vision.

Art must be outstanding examples
of the media, and aesthetically pleasing.
Multiple Impressions, Ltd.

The most influential commercial galleries are the most selective. By the time they become interested in an artist, he or she has probably had several one-person exhibitions. My advice is to develop a strong body of work. Build your assets and present your strengths. The more you bring to the table – awards, grants, positive reviews and a list of buyers or prospective buyers – the more leverage you have with the gallery.

Many dealers' decisions are influenced by the advice of colleagues. Establish as many relationships as possible with the artists who are already in the gallery, and curators, critics, collectors or other dealers who are in the gallery's sphere of influence.

If a gallery states that it is not aggressively looking at new artists' materials, but you feel your work is appropriate for them, instead of sending a bulk of materials, send one or more striking color photographs or a color brochure. Indicate that you would be pleased to send more materials if needed. Invite them to visit your studio. Keep them on your mailing list and abreast of your exhibitions. By keeping the lines of communication open, when the opportunity arises for them to add artists you will have already laid the groundwork.

> *We are taking on few,
> if any, new artists in the foreseeable future.*
> Hoorn-Ashby

Don't be easily discouraged. With the confidence of knowing that you would be an asset to a gallery, you should be making the selection with the utmost care, thoroughness and attention to detail. Pursue the galleries that are most appropriate, without placing too much emphasis on depending on any gallery for your success. If you focus on self-promotion and build a solid career history, the right galleries will be there for you when the time is right and you have acquired leverage.

When approaching galleries, don't think of it as a "pass" or "fail" situation. If the gallery doesn't accept your work on your first attempt, ask why, and for any ideas they may have about which galleries might be interested. Use the experience to gain some information. They may want you to submit your materials again at a later date – to see how your work develops.

Galleries often say they're "not looking" because they have shows scheduled a year or two in advance and are focused on their current projects. They are also probably inundated with materials being sent to them by artists who don't research carefully. My experience has proven galleries "are looking" at the right work that comes their way and are eager to discover something they can work with.

There is another reason not to jump off the Brooklyn Bridge if a gallery rejects you. There are many artists who are enjoying successful careers without having any gallery representation. They have preferred to use their energy in developing relationships with individual art buyers, private dealers and art consultants.

Your goal should be to nurture many professional relationships, unless you have an exclusive agreement with one gallery that offers strong, consistent sales, because it would be futile, otherwise, to rely on one source of income. For example, you may have your slides with the O.I.A. (a non-profit artists organization whose Slide Registry is used by curators and dealers seeking unaffiliated artists), as well as having materials with Images Gallery (a SoHo gallery that has corporate clients), Marlena Greene (a private dealer and curator) and InvestinArt (a corporate art firm that places many emerging artists in corporate collections). You may have your works on paper at Markel Sears Works on Paper and your sculpture with The Sculpture Center.

Contrary to rumor, you don't have to move to New York in order to be exhibited by a New York gallery. However, unless you have someone you know very well serving as your representative in the same locale as the gallery, do not make a commitment with a gallery without seeing it and the owner face-to-face.

Use Protection

When I meet an artist who is misty-eyed with the hope of finding the gallery of his or her dreams, I am reminded of John, a major artist whom I met at a gallery opening, shortly before his death. He asked me if I could recommend a gallery for him. This surprised me, since I assumed he was still represented by one of the leading uptown blue-chip galleries. I learned that John's earlier work was selling in the high five figure range in the secondary market, in which case the artist was not receiving a penny from them, and the gallery wouldn't take on his new work. This left him with a lot of inventory.

This trusting, kind man went to his grave financially poor. Why? Because he relied on the gallery to take care of business for him and he failed to provide for himself. I regret that I didn't meet him earlier to help him avoid his pathetic final few years.

Take care of your art and protect it during every step of your career. Select your gallery wisely and keep a close contact with your dealers. Don't put all of your faith in one gallery. Be careful that you do not become so blinded by your present situation – no matter how good it is – that you fail to make plans for the future.

A verbal contract isn't worth
the paper it's written on.
Louis B. Mayer

Before you begin a relationship with a dealer, you should discuss and agree upon a range of issues – from the duration of the representation to their payment procedure – and get a written contract. It is always best to iron out any disagreements in the beginning rather than having to dispute them later with feelings of resentment and confusion. In many business relationships, it is not necessarily intentional dishonesty that causes problems as much as the misinterpretation of a verbal agreement or the absence of communication.

A list of important items to establish with a dealer are offered in my book *Presentation Power Tools For Fine Artists*. I also recommend that you purchase a book on legal documents for visual artists, such as *Business and Legal Forms for Fine Artists* by Tad Crawford. Since many galleries use a contract that their lawyers have drafted to protect their interests, not yours, it is essential for you to obtain legal counseling before signing a contract.

Before establishing a relationship with any gallery or art professional, check their references through the Better Business Bureau and Attorney General's office. Contact the artists organizations in their area and ask if they have received any complaints. If the gallery is located in New York you may contact me to inquire about its reputation.

Artist shall contribute $6,500 upon the signing of this agreement at his/her share of financial responsibility...
From A New York Gallery Contract

Paying to Show

On a regular basis I receive calls and letters from artists on the subject of New York galleries that charge artists fees to exhibit their work. These fees can be as high as several thousand of dollars, simply for the privilege of hanging their work on a wall. This is a subject I have discussed, repeatedly and passionately, in my seminars and articles. I am sure that I will be responding to these questions for as long as there are artists in need of exposure and galleries that operate in this manner.

In this regard, I am not referring to cooperative galleries, also known as artist-run galleries, which are operated by, and for, artists, and charge membership fees. Nor do I consider galleries that are on under the auspices of non-profit organizations to be included in this category, even if they ask for a financial contribution. For example, New York Artists Equity Association operates Broome Street Gallery on the premises of their office space, in SoHo, which they rent to individual artists and organizations to defray their costs.

My objection is to the opportunistic gallery owner whose intention is to profit from the artists' fees rather than the sales of art, and who pretends to have the same distinction as a legitimate gallery. Legitimate galleries focus on producing buyers and recognition for their artist, not preying on the vulnerability of artists who desire a gallery exhibition, at practically any cost.

In the least desirable instances, the fees the artists pay simply cover the rental of wall space (the artist is actually subleasing space, in my opinion), and the artist may be expected to pay for other exhibition-related expenses. Some of the galleries justify their fees by including advertisements in national magazines and color brochures and by sending out postcards, but they usually exaggerate their costs.

I have seen a number of fee-paid galleries come and go over the last two decades. In fact, I have been called upon more than once to intervene on behalf of the artist in order to retrieve money or art work.

I have looked at every angle of this scenario in order to be a fair judge, especially when I know that so many artists have chosen to exhibit in fee-paid galleries. I wish I could say that of the dozens of artists I know who have taken this route, I have heard positive responses, but I have not.

Most artists have complained that their fees far outweighed the benefits. Furthermore, many individuals who operate these galleries lack the necessary skills to be an effective agent for the artists. They often behave in a condescending manner toward the artist, acting as though they were doing them a favor, instead of giving him or her the respect they deserve. It amazes me that artists tolerate more abuse from galleries than they would ever accept in their personal relationships. My opinion on this issue remains firm. They do more harm than good to an artist's self-esteem and career.

Consider this: if you pay a dealer a sizable fee, which covers a substantial part of the overhead expenses, how much incentive is there for the dealer to sell the work? Why do these types of galleries need to regularly advertise "Call for Artists" in art magazines? Good news travels fast through word of mouth. If the gallery was generating good will for the artists who paid to show with them, they wouldn't need to advertise aggressively.

Whether or not you pay for a show is your choice. An artist's expectations from this kind of exhibition is often very different from the reality. Make decisions with your head, not your emotions. Examine the pitfalls as well as the advantages of exhibiting your work in this manner. Remember, the gallery's commitment you hold only lasts until the next group of paying artists arrive.

Galleries that charge fees for exhibitions seem to have multiplied in recent years. My file containing copies of their contracts has grown. Many of them have become very adept at luring the artist into the palm of their hand with the right buzz-words and sales psychology. Their advertisements appear where artists are likely to look for opportunities, and they also buy artist mailing lists. So, chances are you've been approached by them.

When faced with the temptation to pay, consider these questions: What do you hope to achieve from this venture? What role will this exhibition play in your overall career objectives? What do the leading critics, gallery owners, artists organizations and fellow artists say about the gallery? How many legitimate reviews has the gallery received?

Get out your calculator. Does your fee (combined with other exhibiting artists), cover a large portion of the gallery's operating expenses? What are your risks for the investment you are making? How much do you have to sell in order to cover your expenses? Don't forget to add up all of your expenses including shipping, insurance, framing and traveling.

Many of you will be tempted to take the risk. If you should acquiesce to a fee-paid gallery, before paying a penny, *get everything that was promised to you in writing.* Hire a lawyer to write up a contract that includes your entitlements such as a partial or full refund if the gallery fails to live up to their end of the agreement.

Surprised? Contrary to what you may have been led to believe, you are entitled to services rendered. You are entitled to ask questions and receive professional respect. If you don't get it, place your checkbook back in your pocket and run! Then write to me about your experience and include the name of the gallery and director. You will not only be doing yourself a favor, but helping other artists.

Artists should refuse to pay galleries to exhibit their work, and devote more time and energy in self-promotion. By eliminating the profits earned at the expense of artists, these dealers would have to either improve their gallery operating skills or find other means of support.

If your work has merit and you are an ambitious self-promoter you could invest your money in other ways, such as printing a brochure to cultivate direct sales, hiring an administrative assistant, or consulting a publicist to build your media exposure. Join a cooperative gallery, hold "Open Studio" events, and make use of the myriad of alternative exhibition spaces in the United States and abroad.

If you want autonomy you may consider one of the New York cooperative galleries or rent an exhibition space, in which you either "sit" your own show or hire a sales attendant. In this situation you have the freedom to establish your own prices, do not have to pay a commission to the gallery, and you may have a one-person exhibition or share the rental with other artists who will also devote time and money to attract visitors and prospective buyers. 2/20 Gallery, which is owned by Miguel Herrera, an artist, has been a low-cost exhibition venue for many artist-curated shows.

Does it Ever Pay to Pay?

If you are an artist from a foreign country, paying for exhibitions may be the norm. If you are starting a career and return to your country as having exhibited in a New York gallery, you may be highly rewarded for this accomplishment. The same may be true for an artist who lives far outside of New York in a small town in the United States. You may also argue that it is difficult and time-consuming to obtain a gallery from a long distance away, and a New York show may give your career a jump-start.

I can recall one rare occasion in which an artist benefited from having a fee-paid exhibition. I gave counsel to Janice, an artist from Germany, who had been receiving several thousands of dollars for her paintings. She asked me to locate a New York gallery in which she could have a show within a few months time. It is very rare, if not impossible for a regular gallery to have an opening within a short period of time. The only gallery that could accommodate her was a large gallery in a prominent street-level location on West Broadway in SoHo, but it required a substantial deposit against sales.

Janice considered the circumstances and decided to proceed. Since she was affluent the financial cost was not placing her at risk. She knew only a handful of people in New York, so she enlisted my services for a mailing list, and publicity and promotion assistance.

The director of the gallery hung an outstanding show and was a gracious hostess at the opening reception. A few of Janice's collectors flew in from Germany and made purchases which covered the gallery fee and my counseling fee. As a result of the exposure in the gallery, Janice was invited to exhibit in a group show at a museum, which added to her credibility and increased the subsequent value of her work. An art dealer on Fifty-Seventh Street whom I had invited offered her a group show. Janice considered it a success, however, the results would not have been the same if she had paid for a vanity exhibition in a different location, without carrying the promotional campaign.

Questions to Ask
Before Taking the Plunge

After you have checked the Better Business Bureau, Attorney General's office and artists organizations for any possible complaints, the following questions should be answered to your satisfaction before exhibiting in *any* gallery – fees or no fees.

Is the gallery genuinely impressed with your work and why? Does the gallery offer you a contract which obligates them to perform specific services *for you* or does the contract serve only to protect *them?*

Do they offer tangible promotional and marketing services? When you ask for specific proofs of past performance, do they respond with concrete evidence?

Do they treat you in a condescending manner as one who should be grateful to them for the opportunity to have a show?

Is the gallery easy to find? What is the appearance and attitude of the gallery and staff? Is the quality of the artwork consistent? Are the sales people courteous and knowledgeable? Is the hanging and lighting properly arranged?

Exhibition: One group show.
10' high x 10' wide wall space.
The non-refundable fee is $1,250.

From A New York Gallery Contract

Visit the gallery routinely over a period of at least two seasons, at different times of the day. Attend their receptions. Compare their style of doing business with successful galleries that are known for building their artists' reputations. Over this period of time, have you observed many qualified buyers visiting the gallery? How would you categorize the attendance at the receptions? Are they predominantly exhibiting artists and their friends and relatives? Or does the gallery have a respected following of art consultants, interior designers, architects, collectors and members of the press?

Does the gallery consistently advertise in art publications for "Call For Artists" and "Competitions"?

If the gallery is offering you extended representation, how many exhibitions are they offering in one year? What are the costs? What month(s) are they offering you? (In New York,

January, February, July and August are the kiss of death.) What else will you receive?

What effort will they make to sell the work? Successful galleries don't just sit back after they hang the art work, relying on walk-in traffic or sales; they generate sales through phone calls, press releases, advertising, mailings and a range of networking activities.

What portion of your fee goes for advertising? What kinds of advertising vehicles – radio, TV, print – do they buy?

Do they permit you to have a role in the decision-making process about where and how they spend *your* money? Are they overstating their costs? Will you have to pay for invitations, receptions, advertising?

Have most of their artists remained with them for more than five years? Or have many artists left to join other galleries? Do you know any artists in the gallery who have had work sold through the gallery? Do they have any complaints?

> *It is no use trying to get me out of*
> *my pessimism about picture-dealing.*
> *I see this peculiar interference with prices*
> *in painting more and more as a sort of traffic*
> *rather like the one in tulips.*
> Vincent van Gogh

Chapter 4

5 Keys to Success
The Building Blocks for Professional Power

1. **Confidence**
2. **Commitment**
3. **Persistence**
4. **Courage**
5. **Change**

> *Great minds have purposes;*
> *others have wishes.*
> Washington Irving

Over the years, as I studied the attitude and behavior of many different successful artists and applied success strategies in my own work, I have observed certain consistencies. It is frequently not the talent an artist has that will attract success, but the unwavering confidence, commitment, persistence, courage and change that help them bring their goals to fruition. This section could easily expand to fill a book of its own. If you read nothing more in this book than this segment, you will have a strong basis for success and prosperity.

You may want to put these keys to success to memory, as I have, and use them as an instant checklist if something goes awry in your career. You will probably find the villain when one of these items has been overlooked or is in short supply.

*You gain strength, courage and confidence
by every experience in which
you really stop to look fear in the face.
You are able to say to yourself,
"I lived through this horror.
I can take the next thing that comes along."
You must do the thing you think you cannot do.*
Eleanor Roosevelt

Confidence

One of the reasons why artists seek my help is to be reassured that they have talent. Certainly, we all look for others for validation and psychological support. But, unless the artist is convinced of his or her own abilities most of the time, the confidence will fade as soon as they encounter rejection.

Without confidence rejection will destroy self-sufficiency and integrity. Confidence is necessary in order to take action and persist in the face of the most difficult challenges. When you watch an Olympic champion, you can see their intense concentration and belief in their ability to excel, and how it propels them forward. The athlete knows that the smallest doubt encumbers his or her performance.

Fear is the enemy of success. You can develop confidence by confronting your greatest fears and exercising muscles to build self-esteem. When faced by an intimidating situation, view it as an opportunity to test and develop your inner strength.

Every achievement is tangible proof that you are capable of attaining any goal you desire. When you accomplish a measure of success, give yourself the proverbial pat on the back. Frame your awards, letters of acceptances and positive reviews and display them in prominent locations in your studio. Read them when you need that extra boost.

A successful artist knows it requires confidence to market and promote him or herself as much as the art. A confident artist speaks about his or her work with passion and enthusiasm to everyone! A confident artist continues to develop an existing innate talent and learns to acquire new skills.

You may not always *feel* confident, but you must at least learn how to *act* confident when you need to, and you will notice that your behavior will affect your attitude. Practice standing erect and speaking with conviction. When you need assurance, visualize a time when you felt self-assured and recreate that feeling of confidence.

Confidence is stimulating and infectious. If you believe in yourself and your work and learn to reflect it, so will others. Recognize those debilitating voices in your head that thwart your confidence and learn to dismiss them. Stop second-guessing your talent and allow your innate gifts to flourish. Do what comes naturally – trust the purity and honesty of your creative expression.

> *If you think you can, you can.*
> *And if you think you can't, you're right.*
> Mary Kay Ash

*Until one is committed, there is hesitancy,
the chance to draw back, always ineffectiveness.
Concerning all acts of initiative,
there is one elementary truth, the ignorance of which
kills countless ideas and splendid plans:
That the moment one definitely commits oneself,
then providence moves too...
Whatever you can do, or dream you can, begin it.
Boldness has genius, power, and magic in it.*
Goethe

Commitment

When your career is going smoothly, it is easy to stay committed to your goals. When sales are steady, you seem to attract more buyers. When your work receives rave reviews, you are inspired to produce more spectacular pieces.

Then – wham! Without warning, your art gets damaged in a flood, your gallery goes bankrupt, or the promised fellowship or grant falls through. The ugly monster of doom hovers over you, grinning and testing your faith and conviction. You may be tempted to give up – but don't!

The brilliant artist Chuck Close is a quadriplegic confined to a wheel chair; he paints with a brush strapped to his wrist. He learned about commitment at a young age when, despite having learning disabilities as a child, he went on to college. Later, as an adult and already established as an artist, he was struck with a sudden illness that left him physically challenged. In the book *Chronicles of Courage* by Jean Kennedy Smith and George Plimpton, he states: "One thing that was clear to me early on was how important it was to have something to do. Something that you're anxious to get back to. I wanted to get back to work because I enjoy what I do. I love making art... It's largely how I see myself. I'm an artist, therefore I have to make art."

> *I believe in listening to cycles.*
> *I listen by not forcing.*
> *If I am in a dead working period, I wait,*
> *though these periods are hard to deal with.*
> *I'll be content if I get started again...*
> Lee Krasner

Commitment, tenacity and perseverance are team players. When a person becomes successful and achieves his or her goals, it is not always attributed to physical prowess, the accumulation of financial wealth, or the level of education. Most of the time it is that intense desire and commitment that make it happen. When we look back on the tragic events in our lives, we realize that we survived in spite of them; if we were wise and courageous, we even triumphed as a result of having faced the task. Committing to a dream means following through with hourly, daily, weekly and monthly activities. Success is not measured in terms of a single event but our strength and endurance to prevail despite the odds.

A successful career begins with a determined effort to be the best artist you can be – whether you receive support from others or not. It requires a steadfast commitment to make sacrifices, compromises, to take risks and to invest substantial amounts of time and money – over and over again.

If you are dedicated to being a professional artist, no matter how busy you are, never put your art on the back burner. In spite of your source of income and family responsibilities, you must make time for the art. Take a sketch book with you to work, draw on the subway or bus, or while you are waiting on line at the post office. Take your camera with you to record images and ideas to later turn into works of art. Learn how to maximize time efficiently. Find time for self-expression, even if you have to wake up one hour earlier. Whatever responsibilities you may have in your life, don't neglect your inner needs for artistic growth or a part of you will die. For an artist, art is nitrogen for the soul.

Commitment requires discipline to work long and hard to create the artwork, to market and promote it, and to carry out the necessary administrative tasks. You must invest the time and money to create and support your art, and this will sharpen your creative and marketing skills. Commitment is required to increase knowledge through a wide range of resources, and to keep abreast of current market conditions, trends and opportunities.

Commitment to your artistic vision gives your art the focus and cohesion required for commercial success. Commitment will give you the vitality to create art – in abundance and with standards of excellence. As you develop these attributes, you will attract the dedication of others who are in positions to help you.

As an artist you must be also committed to preserving the welfare of all artists. Join forces with others and cooperate as a team member; you will become individually strengthened by sharing mutual aspirations. Anything involving group interaction requires a primary commitment from all the members. They must participate fully to attain the goals of the organization.

Commitment to your career often means sacrificing personal pleasures. A promise to meet with a dealer or finish a project and adhere to a deadline may cause you disappointment as well as others. Commitment to a career goal often requires that you say no to situations and people that are blocking your path.

Is competency enough for an artist?
All artisans or craftsmen should be proficient
at their trade, but an artist must reach for the stars.
At this time, on the brink of a new century we must
reach beyond mere competency and "go for the gold"
using our hard won abilities to transcend
the level of a journeyman painter.
We must use our heart, mind, and emotional spirit
to bring to the world of art
freedom to experiment, combine mediums,
and be emotional and exciting.
Show me not how facile you can be –
show me your spirit and let your craft shine through
with vitality and vibrancy.
Be brave, and, as someone better than me said,
if you make a mistake, make it a BIG one.
Sidney H. Hermel,
Artist, and President, Pastel Society of America

Persistence

Simply stated, persistence pays. Ask any artist who finally achieves a major break-through in their career after working very hard and devotedly for extended periods of time. They didn't give up after the phone call wasn't returned or the project fell through or several galleries rejected their work. They learned that it requires tremendous effort to find the right connection. The artist who gives up after a few tries is opening up a position for the next artist in line.

Persistence is required to bring your art to the public, through exhibitions, media exposure and the circulation of your promotional materials – to new prospects as well as to existing audiences. Continued efforts will earn your rightful position in the art world. When you are in the game long enough and everyone is accustomed to you and your style and your contributions, opportunities will find their way to you.

A major component in your creative process and your career activities is your ability to persevere and overcome artistic challenges. It leads the artist to develop a strong body of work that reflects purpose and focus – a solid, mature execution of your artistic vision. In today's society the artist who lacks tenacity and grit to tough it out to the end if often rejected on the grounds of appearing unprofessional, unfocussed, and unmarketable.

Consistency is the ability to focus on doing your work well over and over again, improving each step of the way. Consistency without redundancy: superior work explores versatility and flexibility within a larger reference.

You will need to persevere especially when your work doesn't receive any praise. Mark Rothko said: "The unfriendliness of society to his activity is difficult for the artist to accept. Yet this very hostility can act as a lever for true liberation." The next time you feel like giving up, recall Robert Frost's words: "The best way *out* is always *through*." Remember these examples of persistence: The Coca-Cola company sold only four hundred Cokes in its first year of business and Dr. Seuss's first book was rejected by twenty-three publishers.

Joseph Campbell said: "The artist must build a structure, not in the way of being of service to society, but in the way of discovering the dynamism of the interior. To nurture your creative aspect, you must put a hermetically sealed retort, so that there is no intrusion, around a certain number of hours each day… and that time must be inviolate."

Courage is doing what you're afraid to do.
There can be no courage unless you're scared.
Eddie Rickenbacker

Courage

Success depends on the courage to act, and courage requires confidence that every opportunity acted upon will lead to more and better ways to learn, grow and prosper.

In an earlier section of this book, I described how Barbara, by exploring the unknown, and having the courage to risk ridicule, developed more confidence and gained more achievements in other areas of her life. The fear of rejection often discourages artists from stretching and testing new grounds. They may set only a few minor goals or none at all. Other artists turn to "vanity" galleries, in which they would rather pay a gallery to exhibit their work than devote time to acquire reputable gallery representation.

If this is you, you should realize you are not alone. Initiate an artist support group with the primary objective of sharing experiences and find solutions to common challenges, including dealing with rejection. With other artists, you may find the courage to make better career choices.

Have the courage to set very high goals. Get out of your comfort zone. Take risks, especially in the face of defeat. Begin by taking one risk each day. Make the phone call, arrange the appointment, throw the paint onto the canvas, break the mold. Living as an artist is the excitement of not knowing what idea will come to you next, or how. The moment you know how, you begin to lose creative spontaneity. Take chances and leaps of faith in the shrouds of mystery. Enjoy the wonders of always beginning anew.

*The real voyage of discovery
consists not in seeking new landscapes,
but in having new eyes.*
Marcel Proust

Change

When you hear the clamor of chimes and the popping of champagne corks with the dawn of a new year, does your whole body sigh with a sense of relief? Do you feel as though you can shed all of last year's mistakes, misfortunes and miseries, and enter a future in which you will be renewed, and totally absolved from all of your past sins and sorrows? Or does the fear of the unknown paralyze you?

When you blow the dust away and begin a clean slate, you should make time to assess your record of successes and failures during the last year. Take a good long look in the large, magnifying mirror in bright daylight. Don't dwell on your mistakes, but use your current position of retrospection to improve your future performance. To see your failures objectively is the opportunity to begin again more intelligently. Take stock, take responsibility and move forward. Enlist friends, fellow artists and mentors to help.

The problems and challenges that have plagued you in the past are the seeds to make constructive and powerful changes. Otherwise, you will be doomed to repeat your mistakes.

Did you lose a gallery, job or grant? Was the loss devastating, or did the experience teach you something more important? Did something unanticipated take you by surprise to another place which turned out to be more rewarding?

*The human tendency prefers
familiar horrors to unknown delights.*
Fred Woodworth

Confront those events that puzzle, confuse, overwhelm and cause you pain. How can you eliminate those negative feelings? What mishap can you prevent? What negative people should you eliminate from your life? Who did you regrettably ignore who deserves an apology?

Also focus on your accomplishments. Which tactics did you apply that were most effective? What must you continue to do in order to increase your achievements? Credit yourself for all of your minor as well as major strides that have made an impact on your career. Applaud yourself for making all of those wise decisions, and continue to take the same positive action that brought you success. Remember, success is more attitude than aptitude.

Heraculitus said: "Nothing endures but change." Complacency is the enemy of growth. It is important to ask yourself periodically: "Am I pursuing my goals *Now*? Do I feel passionate about the kind of art I am producing *Now*? These questions will either comfort you or provoke you to make profound changes.

As your life changes, so will your goals and priorities. A periodic checkup will help you to see if your life's purpose and current situation are complementary.

The downfall for many is their fear of change. Change has a considerable psychological impact on the human mind. To the fearful it is threatening because it suggests things might get worse. A person's character and frame of mind determines how receptive he or she is to making changes and how he or she reacts when change is imposed.

A reluctance to change is one of the major culprits of aging. If you want eternal youth, embrace change with a positive attitude. Be receptive to it by keeping abreast of emerging trends, technological advances, new art forms, techniques, new ways of exhibiting and marketing your art and new "artspeak." Read leading-edge art magazines from around the globe. Avoid the temptation to immediately dismiss anything new and different. Look for new ways to bring your art to new audiences. Surround yourself with youthful, innovating and exuberant people who welcome change.

Things do not change; we change.
Henry David Thoreau

Powerful Questions that Lead to Change

1. What are my priorities today? This year? This lifetime?
2. What positive step can I take to better my career?
3. How am I procrastinating and why?
4. Am I currently creating what my heart tells me to?
5. What toxic relationship must I end?
6. How am I sabotaging my career?
7. How much money do I want to earn from my art this year?
8. How can I channel my talent to serve humanity?
9. Who deserves an apology from me? Gratitude? Forgiveness?
10. How do I want to be remembered?
11. Which new medium should I explore? Invent?
12. What should I be teaching others about art and artists?

Chapter 5

Relationships Create Your Power Base

*Dismiss any fear of being robbed
of your creativity and share it willingly.
Share your art, resources and ideas,
with artists, other individuals,
organizations and communities.
Remember, you only really own
that which you give away.*
Renée Phillips

The single most valuable part of your career may be the relationships you develop. Think of key events in your professional life that marked a turning point – your first sale, a great exhibition, or receiving a distinguished honor or award. When you examine the circumstances, you will realize that it would not have occurred without the help of someone – an artist, a gallery owner, an art buyer or a juror – making a decision or taking an action that would forever change the course of your career.

In the highly competitive artistic community, much of your success relies on the support and camaraderie of fellow artists, art writers and critics, grant givers, dealers, collectors and other individuals. Collectors recommend artists to dealers. Galleries seek the advice of the artists they represent when adding new artists. Grant givers require endorsements from art leaders. Art writers obtain story ideas from other art professionals. Simply, the more contacts you have, the more forerunners who know about you and your talents, the more opportunities you will have.

Selection process: 75% of the artists are selected from professional referrals; 20% from slides sent to the gallery; and 5% from art seen in exhibitions or artists' studios.
Denise Bibro

In today's professional world, building relationships through networking is a survival skill. The more time you spend in your art community, you will notice that it actually consists of a relatively small group of people who play musical chairs. The division among art careers used to be much more defined. In recent years, however, the roles of artists, art dealers, critics and collectors have become interchangeable. The artist is often a curator, the collector is considered a consultant, and the art dealer frequently comes from a background that contains a mixture of any of these. In this respect, it is wise to cultivate strong ties with those people who are committed to being involved in the art world for the long haul. And since that is not always obvious, you shouldn't burn any bridges along the way.

In the process of creating *New York Contemporary Art Galleries: The Complete Annual Guide*, we asked every dealer about their selection process and offered multiple choices: How many do they select from professional referrals? How many artists are selected from slides and other materials they receive? How many artists are selected from seeing their work in exhibitions and artists' studios? Many galleries state that most of the artists are selected from professional referrals.

Although galleries often discover artists from slides sent through the mail, an introduction to the gallery by a mutual friend will increase your chances. Having friends in positions to help you may not guarantee success, but the windows and doors will crack open a bit easier. Once you step inside, it's up to you.

> *We must, indeed, all hang together,*
> *or most assuredly we will all hang separately.*
> Benjamin Franklin

The Art of Networking

The art of networking is simply about establishing relationships with people as a result of searching for mutual benefits and by making yourself useful. The best relationships are nurtured through respect and over a period of time.

You may have noticed that for some artists, networking comes naturally. They have acquired some basic social skills. They attend a lot of the gallery openings and always seem to meet or already know the most important people in the room. Their antenna is always up. An artist who is successfully climbing the ladder is usually an artist who has developed many personal and professional relationships, through his or her integrity, helpfulness and, by being, reliable. These individuals know the importance of building their reputation through others.

Networking is not about coveting as many connections as possible for selfish gain. Good networkers know the art of approaching others with an anticipation of exploring shared or complementary interests. A good networker is a good listener, and he or she is open to other people's opinions, ideas and is able to interact with different types of people. Artists who are egotistical, argumentative, or overly sensitive to criticism may have difficulty in this area.

Networking is an activity that takes place everywhere with everyone. The opportunities to make new contacts are endless. Some of the most productive contacts come from chance encounters – waiting for the bus or subway, in the grocery checkout line, in the doctor's waiting room, at the post office, in an elevator, at a place of worship or at your child's school.

Opportunities multiply as they are seized.
SunTzu

Be prepared to network. Carry an ample supply of business cards and visual "handouts" such as postcards or business cards that feature an image of your work, and keep them in a clean, protective case. After you exchange cards with someone, jot down a reminder on the back of that person's card such as where you met, what you discussed, possible exhibition or sales opportunities, and how you should follow up.

Record new acquaintances and contacts in a rolodex, computer file or index cards. Set up whatever system works best for you to follow up and nurture your new contacts. Use every opportunity to send a personal note, a thank you, a congratulations, or any relevant and useful information for the individual.

Looking for ways to increase your contacts? Reach beyond your studio. Attend gallery receptions. Go to lectures, symposiums and events held in museums and art centers. Visit the art expositions in major cities. Take a job as an assistant to a well-established artist in your medium. Take a job in a gallery. Get involved in your community and with charity organizations. Offer to make a donation of part of your proceeds from art sales. Volunteer to work on a committee of your art organization, as this position will place you in touch with a members of the business community. Volunteer to work on the events committee of your art organization. Organize lectures with leading curators, dealers and critics. Contact a famous artist you admire and ask to visit them in their studio, and return the invitation.

One way of meeting important people in the art world is to work in a related field – as a curator, public speaker or art writer. For example, several artists are on the editorial board of *Manhattan Arts International* magazine. They gain access to private press receptions. As writers, they have a forum to express their views. They make valuable contacts by interviewing leading art dealers, museum curators and renowned artists. They enjoy uninterrupted quality time, sometimes hours for one interview, to obtain vital information, and to speak about their own work. The experience has led to career advancement.

A practice I have developed over the years is the art of being a good professional matchmaker. I enjoy bringing two people together whom I think would benefit from knowing each other. It is very exciting when my introductions lead to professional alliances and friendships. I encourage you to develop this very simple and rewarding habit. It's contagious.

Networking is a reciprocal process. It works best with the attitude that it is as rewarding to give information, resources, advice and referrals as it is to receive. Dismiss any fear of being robbed of your creativity and share it willingly. Share your art, resources and your ideas, not only with artists, but also with other professionals, organizations and communities. Remember, you only really own that which you give away.

*All in all the creative act
is not formed by the artist alone;
the spectator brings the work in contact with
the external world by deciphering
and interpreting its inner qualifications and thus
adds his contribution to the creative act.*
Marcel Duchamp

Getting Psyched to Network

It's easy to become isolated when you work at home. Force yourself to get out and mingle with others who can provide a business support structure for you. For many artists who prefer to work quietly alone in the studio, the idea of having to attend an opening reception and mingle with strangers can be excruciating. If trying to avoid the unpleasant experience is holding you back from attending events that could be helpful to your career, you can "psyche" yourself into the mood.

Observe the intensity of feeling when you are excited about a new direction with your work, or an upcoming exhibition. Put yourself into that state of mind when you are faced with having to meet new people, show your work to a new gallery, or attend your opening reception. Exercise a range of animated motion in your body movements, be alert and hold your head high. Your mental state will be improved, and you will appear confident and enthusiastic.

If you sit or stand in one position all day creating work, you should stop occasionally and vary your physical exercise with activity. Try deep breathing and faster movement to vitalize yourself and prepare for action when the situation calls for it.

*It is not so much our friends' help that helps us
as the confident knowledge that they will help us.*
Epicurus

Camaraderie

Your rolodexes may be overflowing with innumerable contact names, but there is nothing like heartfelt camaraderie to take you to a higher spiritual plateau. Camaraderie develops through mutual trust and shared missions. When such a bond is formed, it is deeply rewarding and empowering. Artists who feel isolated don't have to look far to find the real intimacy that they need is right within the artist population. With a staggering number of hundreds of thousands of artists graduating each year, if nothing else, there is solace and strength in numbers.

Unfortunately, many artists look upon their fellow artists as competitors, not allies. It takes confidence, commitment, persistence and courage to benefit the most from forming concrete relationships with each other.

You may argue that being an artist is a highly competitive profession; there are more artists than there are venues to accommodate them. However, there are also limitless opportunities if you dare imagine and create them – enough for everyone. Artists who share this belief exude a spirit of cooperation and enthusiasm. They take an assertive approach to make changes in their careers and reach out to help other artists. They may curate a group exhibition to showcase artists who work in a similar direction, or propose a group community arts mural project, or organize a lecture or workshop program, or launch a cooperative gallery. They often work tirelessly without pay or accolades to improve the status of all artists, not merely their own.

Donna Marxer, is such an artist. She is a recognized painter, writer, public speaker and arts activist. She is the Executive Director of Artists Talk On Art, a 24-year-old panel series in New York City dedicated to addressing the issues of artists. She is a board member of New York's Organization of Independent Artists as well as Founder and Chairman of "Quarterly Report," a feminist roundtable. She also serves as a juror for national exhibitions and was recently a visual arts panelist for the Ohio State Arts Council. As a highly respected arts writer, Marxer was a regular columnist for *Art Calendar* magazine in the 90s and has been a contributor to national art publications since the 60s. As a labor of love, she is contributor of a series of oral interviews with older women artists for the National Archives of American Art. She offers this sage advice:

> *First and foremost, artists should*
> *give up self pity and do their work.*
> *Despair and fear of failure must be*
> *fought against as the enemies of creativity.*
> *Then, we artists should help one another,*
> *share information instead of hugging secrets.*
> *When we give out instead of hoarding our hurts,*
> *the pain becomes manageable and*
> *we are also doing some good for others.*

The Power of Arts Organizations

I feel very strongly about the importance of joining and supporting artists organizations. Their value has increased since our society has become increasingly more depersonalized. Artists suffer if they spend too much time isolated from other artists. They need to share values, convictions, ambitions and problem-solving. They need a support group for creative and spiritual development. Today, many online chat groups attract and connect bridges among artists world-wide.

It is an artist's obligation to join forces with like-minded creative individuals to actively improve conditions for future generations of artists. That includes having a collective voice through petitions, writing letters to government officials and speaking at community forums.

You can find the support you need in groups of any size. There are regional, local, national and international groups from which to choose. An artist's organization can supply information about techniques, business and economic changes in the art world, as well as a diverse range of opportunities that are available. Many offer great discounts on insurance, rental cars, art books, art supplies and other business expenses. Many organizations publish newsletters and have websites which offer communication links and resources. Some organizations focus on providing educational information for members who are concerned about self-promotion, marketing, portfolio presentation, pricing and finding customers. Others meet often for slide shows and to critique each other's work. Still others join forces to promote a specific medium, and the emphasis is placed on raising the level of recognition of the group, rather than the individual members.

*An effective organization has a purpose
that is shared by all its members and
to which they will willingly commit their efforts.
People working together can do almost anything.*
James L. Hayes

Successful artists often select a variety of artists organizations that fulfill different needs: one for exhibitions, another for intellectual stimulation, and another for their social and professional activities.

Before joining a group, decide what you want the organization to provide for you. Do you want to join a club for social reasons? To gain camaraderie? To benefit from a casual networking situation? Join arts organizations that share your vision and are primarily comprised of like-minded, positive individuals. As a member project a feeling of alliance. Set group goals and make a commitment to strive to help each other reach your objectives most successfully.

Take a tip from John F. Kennedy and ask not what your organization can do for you, but what can you do for your organization. As a member, volunteer to work on a committee or single project. You will develop skills, knowledge and connections. For example, having a position on the publicity committee of your art organization will put you in touch with the press. And, if you volunteer to work on the events committee of your art organization, you can contact leading curators, dealers and critics to organize a panel discussion or series of lectures.

Regina Stewart, Executive Director of New York Artists Equity Association, offers these words of wisdom:

*Join a nonprofit arts organization
and help the greater community of artists.
Volunteer to work on one of the organization's projects.
Volunteering is personally and professionally rewarding.
Your help benefits the organization and
it enables you to meet not only other artists
but the people who support and legislate the arts.
New contacts and expanded knowledge
are continuing sources of new and exciting options.*

Joining an artists organization is the quickest way for an artist to feel less like an outsider if he or she are new to a community. It is also one of the best methods for an artist who is beginning their career to develop an exhibition history.

Once you make a decision,
the universe conspires to make it happen.
Ralph Waldo Emerson

When you decide what is important to you, and there are no local groups to fill your needs, consider starting your own. When I formed Artopia, the main purpose was to organize exhibitions for under-recognized artists. But also important was a forum to share ideas. In addition to the multi-media exhibitions, I held regular membership meetings and published a monthly newsletter. We invited other professionals to become supporting members, such as lawyers, marketing professionals, and members of the press, and we gained tremendously from their expertise. In return for their involvement, they received members' discounts on artist members' art work and invitations to our social events and private visits to artists' studios.

It is equally important to know when it is time to move on, such as when you realize that the group does not share your artistic standards or career goals, or if you feel that your contributions are not appreciated. Realize that your time and energy are valuable, bow out gracefully, and seek more appropriate groups. You may also find what you need is the camaraderie you gain from a handful of artists whom you respect and meet with regularly, without the need for the structure of an official organization.

*Without him
I would have given up.*
Pierre Auguste Renoir on Monet

Go! Go! Get a Coach!

Everyone needs a coach to cheer them on for all the small and major achievements in their lives. A coach with whom you can test new ideas and get an objective opinion is critical.

To accomplish your goals as a successful artist, you need to build a support system in your work and in your personal life. Seek out positive and motivational role models and become a positive role model for others. Establish relationships with one or more mentors. Your mentor or coach can consist of family members or friends. Meet with them or call them regularly to report progress, obtain advice and receive encouragement. Let them know what you are doing, and how they and others will benefit from the results you want to produce. Invite them to lend their support however they can. Let others know how they can be of help to you and accept their help with joyful appreciation. Eagerly return the support to them.

An example of having a friend coach you is to call them when you're stuck. You might say: "I have to get this project done, but I can't seem to generate the interest or stamina." Your friend would listen and show empathy, then remind you how much you would benefit once the project was completed, or help you break it down into bite-size pieces. Your friend could also call you every hour to coach you along. Don't forget to keep your conversations related to the project and no longer than five minutes, otherwise you might find yourself procrastinating and discussing other irrelevant topics.

*A consultant is an ordinary man
away from home giving advice.*
Oscar Wilde

You can also hire a professional career coach. Coaches are becoming one of the fastest growing service providers of this decade. Perhaps it was Anthony Robbins who started the wave, or maybe corporate downsizing placed a lot of corporate managers on unemployment lines which may have led to a plethora of new coaches. When seeking a good coach, look for someone who listens attentively, has compassion for your feelings, reserves judgment, and motivates you to take the best possible action to reach your most desired results. The best professional coach will have experience in business and the business of art, psychology, and transformational work. A good career coach will focus on helping you develop tools with which you can solve your problems by yourself, and will not try to make you depend upon him or her to solve them for you.

Until the name became a 90s buzzword, I was not aware that I had been an artist' coach for several years. As a career advisor and coach, I provide the structure, direction, and support to counsel and encourage artists to persist in their goals and connect with their own spirit. I offer them tools to help them overcome roadblocks and get them back on track when they fall off. Most of the coaching I provide is on the phone.

An example of a coaching session is when Donna called me minutes after leaving a gallery where she had an appointment to present her work. She was unsure about whether the appointment went satisfactorily. I asked her to explain the events as they occurred, while I helped her to separate the actual events from her interpretations of the facts and her emotional responses. As it turned out, the appointment went better than she had thought. I then gave her advice on how to proceed with the gallery. By eliminating the emotional quotient of apprehension, I led her to a quick and positive resolution where she could be productive. Needless to say, it saved her time and unnecessary anxiety.

In recent months, I have had to curtail my private counseling in order to focus on writing this book, therefore, the demand for my workshops has increased. I have observed many of the same artists attending every one of my workshops. When I ask them why, they tell me they come, not only for the information I provide, but the shot of adrenaline they receive from me and from other artists in the workshop. It coaches them to stay motivated and on track as they pursue their goals.

The stresses and frustrations that affect all human beings are felt more strongly by the artist, who is more sensitive to all stimuli. That is why it is important to reach out to each other and generally supportive individuals who understand the special needs of the artist.

When artists are faced with creative blocks, fear of rejection, chronic frustration, depression or anxiety a motivational workshop will not suffice. They can, however, find the treatment they need through psychotherapy. Sandra Indig is a New York artist, arts therapist and analytic psychotherapist. She offers individual counseling in addition to "Creativity / Creative Process Groups" for visual and performing artists, writers and poets. Among many things, she provides a safe, supportive atmosphere in which artists can explore issues, release blocked energy, bridge the gap between private space to public venue, and change habitual, unproductive behavior. She says, "I encourage the individual artist to face internal blocks which tend to inhibit full expression of his or her talent." She, and many other professionals in her field are offering a service of tremendous benefit for artists who need short-term therapy to help them through a critical time, or long-term assistance to resolve debilitating issues.

Chapter 6

Where Have All The Women Gone?

Historically, women have either been excluded from the process of creating the definitions of what is considered art or allowed to participate only if we accept and work within existing mainstream designations.
Judy Chicago

Staggering Statistics

I am still reeling from an experience I had recently. It began when I received an invitation from Women Executives in Public Relations (a very influential organization of top women in the field), to be a panelist on the subject of the "Status of Women in Fine Arts" at their annual luncheon.

To fully prepare, I began "bean counting" from the 1999 Edition of *New York Contemporary Art Galleries* to determine how many women gallery owners existed in New York (about 20 to30%) and how many women artists were represented by New York galleries (also about 30%).

The ratio of male/female artists represented by the gallery was one of the 40 questions which we asked more than 760 New York gallery owners and directors in the preparation of the book. Some of the dealers resented the question. Others ignored it. Others spontaneously replied with the politically correct response "50/50" and when asked to name four of their artists most often listed three or four men. When they responded with a real number, it was usually 30% women.

There are a few New York galleries that show only women artists, such as A.I.R., Ceres, and SoHo 20. Steinbaum Krauss Gallery is proud of the fact that most of its artists were women. But that is an exception to the rule. New York is also the home of outstanding women's art organizations including Catharine Lorillard Wolfe Art Club, New York Society of Women Artists, National Association of Women Artists, Pen and Brush Club, and Professional Women Photographers.

To obtain a nationwide overview in all areas of Fine Art, I contacted the Archive Dept. of the National Museum of Women in the Arts in Washington, DC. They faxed me Eleanor Dickinson's *1998 Statistical Survey of Gender Discrimination in the Visual Art Field*, which contains copious data derived from U.S. universities, museums, census bureaus, and the Bureau of Labor Statistics, etc. from1960-1997. What an eye-opener! It revealed that most changes for women in fine arts occurred during 1960s-70s. Since then, not much has improved. In the 1998 U.S. census, 46% of the 251,000 painters and sculptors are women, and 56% of fine art degree holders are women. However, there is no correlation between education and economic equality; 72% of those who hold art faculty positions are men; and women comprise only 39% of the artists earning a living from their art. In 1997, women earned 75cents for every $1 men earned. In addition, 2/3 of the artists receiving art grants and fellowships are men. Conclusion: Although a great deal of money is made through the arts, the artists are poorly paid and women artists are paid less than men. Although nearly half of trained available art teachers are women, only 30% are hired, and often in lower ranks.

Not surprisingly, solo and group shows in U.S. Museums are given primarily to men – 70% to be sure. However, the saddest statistic is how poorly women artists are represented in art textbooks. Overall: 3.2% women and 96.8% men. The 1997 Edition of H.W. Janson's *History of Modern Art* contained 444 men and 31 women. So, where can women artists find role models? Are women invisible to most people in power?

You might ask, "Are women artists simply less talented?" The answer is "No!" In juried competitions, when the gender is not revealed to the jurors, the results are closer to 50%/50%.

After sharing these statistics at the panel discussion, I offered some suggestions to the guests: Since women artists are poorly represented in galleries, make an effort to find them and buy their work; place their work in major auctions to drive their values up (a tactic the big boys use); offer to counsel women artists in the areas of public relations; recommend qualified women for jobs in fine art institutions; volunteer to help women artists, women artist organizations and women art galleries; and serve on their advisory boards. Also, write and speak about discrimination against women and all minorities.

Howardena Pindell wrote *The Heart of the Question,* a compelling book that exposes discrimination in the art world. The book succinctly states:

> *There is a closed circle which links the museums, galleries, auction houses, collectors, critics and art museums which systematically excludes minorities.*

Which is to say, if you are a woman of color, you are doubly disadvantaged!

*A woman artist must be capable
of making the primary sacrifices.*
Mary Cassatt

Perception of the Woman/Mother

One of the reasons why women artists fail to obtain gallery or museum representation is that once a woman becomes a mother, she is considered to be less devoted to her career. The truth is, breast feeding and child rearing take time away from creating art. If a female artist with young children is struggling financially to pursue her career, she has little resources and time to promote herself and market her work. Few women artists have the resources to hire nannies and studio assistants. If you are poor or middle class and a single parent with young children, you have to fight hard to sustain any career at all. The resumes of mothers reflect time lapses between exhibitions, commissions, grants and sales. These inconsistencies cannot be hidden and are frequently interpreted as professional flaws, and the artist is considered too much of a financial risk. It is no surprise that when you recall many of the women artists who achieved success, such as Mary Cassatt, Georgia O'Keefe, Judy Chicago, and Frida Kahlo, they were not mothers.

At a certain age, women are often seen as having raging hormonal systems that destroy their credibility. It is necessary for women, more than men, to show that they are good decision-makers, and are reliable, emotionally secure and committed. Fortunately, we have herbal remedies, estrogen replacement therapy, and nutritional supplements to help us as menopause strikes.

If you are a mother you owe it to yourself and your loved ones to fully develop your potential, even if it means sacrificing some home-cooked meals. Ask others to help you, so you can plan creative time and time to promote your career. It is important to strengthen your own position, as well as support other talented women artists, and to serve as a positive role model for future generations of women art professionals.

> *Any woman who has a career and a family automatically*
> *develops something in the way of two personalities,*
> *like two sides of a dollar bill, each different in design...*
> *Her problem is to keep one*
> *from draining the life of the other.*
> Ivy Baker Priest

A New Generation and Changes to Come

As bad as conditions for women may seem, we are in a better place than a century ago. For example, for decades women gallery owners have been prevalent, but women were scarce in the top echelons of the museums. However, conditions are changing. According to a recent survey of the Association of Art Museum Directors, the overall trustee composition among its membership was 62% male and 38% female. Diversification has become a prime goal of many museum boards. Women with the right credentials are increasingly receiving consideration for top museum-management positions. The old-boy network may still exist but is not impenetrable.

The National Museum of Women in the Arts in Washington, DC has made many contributions, "to forge ahead in bringing recognition to women artists of yesterday, today and tomorrow…" And, many women artists are receiving support from organizations such as Anonymous Was A Women, which was established in response to the elimination of fellowships by the NEA. In 1998, it awarded $25,000 to women artists over 30 years of age.

Surveys prove that positive changes occur through pressure, public exposure and protests such as those conducted by the Guerrilla Girls in NYC and California. We need to apply more pressure; we all have a responsibility to foster change.

> *I believe that it is crucial for women artists*
> *to situate ourselves in the context of our own gender,*
> *class, and ethnic histories and struggles*
> *rather than in relationship to male histories.*
> Judy Chicago

Many women artists of the new generation whom I have interviewed are placing their marriages on hold for awhile in favor of pursuing their careers. The child-bearing period has been extended and women are taking advantage of the time it requires to establish themselves. I have observed a predominance of women in attendance at my workshops on the business of art. They are generally seeking career guidance with more focus and assertiveness than their mothers and grandmothers.

The March-April issue of *Manhattan Arts International* is titled "Making Art Herstory in Manhattan" and is devoted to women in fine arts. In conjunction with this special issue we hold a reception in NYC to honor them. It offers an opportunity for all of us – men and women – to feel united, share our vision and make plans for future endeavors. Celebrations such as this are occurring throughout the United States during March, Women's History Month. Get involved!

Chapter 7

Taking Care of Business:
The Role of
The Artrepreneur

*As the old saying goes,
good work, good pay.*
Giotto

The successful artist of the new millennium is what I call an Artrepreneur, a rare combination of artist and business person – each artist finding his or her own balance between the two.

If you decide to create art and keep it as a hobby, then you don't have to deal with the business side of art. On the other hand, if you are like most artists and want to sell your work for a price, then you must prepare to assume the role of an entrepreneur. In the beginning, you should expect to work like any other small businessperson: eighteen hours each day, seven days a week. To sell your work, you must make people aware of you and your work, determine your market, attract influential people, take advantage of opportunities and focus on your income and the results. If you take the time to take care of your career you will earn more time for creating your art.

*What lies behind us and what lies before us
are tiny matters compared to what lies within us.*
Ralph Waldo Emerson

During the past two decades, there have been vast changes in the artist's relationship to the business of art. There are many reasons to feel positive about the future. Roles and relationships have evolved with changing economic conditions. There is a growing intimacy between the artist and the art buyer. After the art boom in the 80s, many art buyers lost faith in the dealers that misdirected them, and they have become more educated consumers. The artist has also become a more educated entrepreneur. The thirst for prosperity is being quenched by a plethora of books about the business of being an artist. Universities and art schools are beginning to offer courses and workshops. More than ever, artist career advisors, like myself, have been invited to present seminars on vital career issues.

Instead of relying solely on galleries to sell their work, a growing number of artists are advertising their artwork in art magazines in which they list their studio addresses and telephone numbers – and now more than ever – their own websites! Artist-curated exhibitions and artist-run galleries have been on the rise. And, artists everywhere are visually transforming corporate spaces, parks, restaurants, book stores and a range of other public and private spaces in which to show and sell their work.

Those of you who are participating in this evolution know the rewarding challenges that face you. You are instrumentally solving the plights of the artists that have existed for decades. As an arts advocate, you are not only improving the art community, but contributing to making the world a more positive and democratic environment.

You should live each day
as you would climb a mountain
Set your goals and strive
to reach the pinnacle of your potential,
but remember to stop and savor
the many spectacular views along the way.

The Rule of Thirds
Creator, Promoter And Administrator
All working together in mutual support and harmony

If you are in the beginning stages of your career, without an agent or gallery that is selling enough of your work on which to live comfortably, you will find yourself in the position of having to be your own marketing and promotion director in addition to being an artist.

Beyond creating your work, you should be setting time aside on a regular basis every week for promotion and administrative work. Your professional career will be divided into three roles: one-third as a creator; one-third marketer and promoter, dealing with getting the clients; one-third as an administrator, taking care of the necessary paper work, telephone calls, mailing, etc. Naturally, these three essential roles will not always be equally divided at the same time. You will define your own schedule and work according to other demands and degrees of success. Once you find effective ways to handle the marketing, promotion and administrative work, you will earn more time for creativity.

One of the best ways to deal with this distasteful reality is to delegate as much of the tedious, unpleasant tasks as possible to others who can do it more efficiently. Depending on your budget, recruit volunteers from your family and friends, senior citizen centers, the local schools and your neighborhood, and hire skilled professionals. Then, roll up your sleeves and take care of the rest. Once you incorporate the necessary tasks into your daily routine, the rewards will be worth the effort, and your feeling of resentment will be replaced with competence.

> *Success Now! means that you hold the key*
> *to your own success, the moment you decide*
> *to believe in your ability to create your destiny.*
> *Success comes as you begin moving*
> *toward a worthwhile goal.*

In a workshop, while I was discussing "The Rule of Thirds" it was obvious that I had struck a nerve with a women in the front row. She began to fidget anxiously and mutter under her breath, until she finally exclaimed aloud: "How can you expect the artist to do everything? Isn't it enough that we make the art? It's not fair!" In response to this sudden outburst, I heard many chuckles of embarrassment from other students, but I also saw several heads nod in agreement. Her response was honest. She had every reason to be upset. I recalled the time in my own life as an artist that I felt the same way.

No one had ever discussed this while she was in art school, or since then, and she was adamantly opposed to this notion. As the first person who ever made this statement to her, my goal was to express my empathy and to carefully explain to her, with the help of several other members of the group, that although we may not like the situation, the sooner we face this reality of life, the better equipped we will be to deal with it and find ways to change it. In my experience, the artists who easily grasp this concept navigate their careers with less frustration.

Particularly in the beginning of your career, before you acquire a consistent sales pattern and a substantial level of recognition, you will be required to invest considerable time, skill and money in the advancement of your career. If applied in equal proportions to your creativity, you will be rewarded with more time to develop creatively! Learn to apply the synergistic power of the three components. They are players on the same team, all working to achieve the same ultimate goal – your success.

*People usually fail when they are on the verge of success.
So give as much care to the end as to the beginning;
Then, there will be no failure.*
Lao Tsu

A Success Story
The Artist Who Applied "The Rule of Thirds"

Lisa contacted me for some advice after amassing a large inventory of paintings in three years. Her paintings depicted Native American history based upon old murals on edifices that were about to be destroyed and replaced by luxury buildings. She had very little business and administrative experience. What she did have, however, was a very solid, inspiring body of work with news value.

She was shocked when I told her she would have to spend the next few months focusing on the marketing phase of her career, thereby sacrificing some studio time. However, she was an artist who understood that the same level of commitment and discipline that she applied to creating her extensive body of work was required to attain the financial and professional goals she desired. She realized that it would be worth the effort to make the short-term sacrifice to reach long-term goals.

> *To have ideas is to gather flowers.*
> *To think is to weave them into garlands.*
> Anne-Sophie Swetchine

After determining her budget, our strategy began by compiling a list of appropriate market leads, consisting of organizations, galleries, institutions, libraries, museums, private individuals and corporations that would be interested in her work. The top of the list started with those she already knew, and was followed by new prospects. In addition to galleries and museums our list included writers, publications, news directors and station managers, who would be interested in the story behind her work. We then created a brochure, wrote cover letters and developed press releases that explained the significance of her project. She made direct calls to 200 individuals and mailed the materials to 750 prospects. She kept records and followed up on the leads.

Armed with a plan, a targeted market, and a large dose of persistence, in about four months Lisa acquired three gallery exhibitions, one museum exhibition, five sales and several commissions. As a result of the publicity efforts, she was profiled in several local and national publications and TV news.

In Lisa's situation, "The Rule of Thirds" consisted of two-and-a-half years as the creator, and only four months as the marketer, promoter and administrator. Not surprisingly, she was very pleased with the results of her efforts. She earned the freedom to return to her studio full time and the resources to hire an assistant to manage the administrative duties.

*I am opposed to millionaires,
but it would be dangerous to offer me the position.*
Mark Twain

Cash Flow

Most entrepreneurs fail because they ignore the importance of understanding their cash flow. So, if you want to succeed in business don't skip this part of the book as much as you may be tempted to do so.

If you are still with me, you might ask: "What is cash flow?" If you look at your next three months projected income or revenue, then compare it with all the expenditures you need to keep the business running, the difference is your cash flow.

Like water, cash sometimes flows abundantly to people, and sometimes it seems to evaporate. You don't want to be adrift at sea without financial security during the unexpected turbulent times. To keep the tides running in your favor, and prepare for rainy days, you need to do some cash forecasting.

What is cash forecasting? To forecast your cash flow future, you need to look at your financial history. Review your records of your sales and expenses for the last three to five years. Determine in which months you experience a particularly high cash flow, and those with an unusually low cash flow. Now, do the same for your expenses. Compare the two. Over a five year period, you will notice definite financial patterns emerge and you will be able to make any necessary corrections. You will want to pay particular attention to those periods in which your expenses are high and your cash flow is low. This procedure will prepare you to prepare for the difficult times and help you to avoid any unfortunate surprises.

Without a plan of action to increase sales and decrease expenses, you will run into some trouble which could have been avoided. This trouble will be worsened by outside factors which you cannot control – such as the economy getting sluggish or your gallery going bankrupt.

If you are a victim of poor cash flow management, you will be powerless in other areas of your career. If you are making a practice of this self-sabotaging habit decide to take control and instill new practices. Establish the important objective of maintaining records of income and expenses. Discover those high and low periods in your business, so you can make the necessary preparations.

Plan your spending. Keep a budget. Constantly compare your budgeted and actual figures to learn where costs are going. As a rule, your operating expenses should be less than twenty percent of your income. That should be an ideal goal.

Eliminate wasteful spending. Keep a detailed journal of your expenses to determine where you can trim costs. Time is money, and eliminating time wasters also saves you money. Don't hesitate to spend money in areas that will help you save time and can help you earn more. An example of a good investment is the purchase of a computer, especially now that they are so affordable and user-friendly. A computer will save you time in maintaining your financial records and mailing list, updating your resume, writing business letters, sending email and obtaining information from the internet.

There are many helpful books and soft ware programs that will help you to manage your money. *Working Solo: The Real Guide to Freedom and Financial Success with Your Own Business*, by Terri Lonier and *Small Business for Dummies* by Eric Tyson and Jim Schell are two of many helpful books available. *(See Appendix.3.)*

*The less one has to do,
the less time one finds to do it in.*
Lord Chesterfield

Time Management

As we approach the new millennium, seasons seem to change more rapidly. Time often appears as our rival in the game of life, in our challenge to capture and control it, get ahead of it and make the most use of it. We try to juggle several balls in the air at the same time – the responsibilities of raising children, caring for an elderly parent, holding down a job – and our need to replenish ourselves with creativity. It is no wonder that stress is the buzzword of the 90s, with a plethora of pills and homeopathic remedies that promises to cure. We need help!

Among the top time wasters are: telephone socializing, junk mail, a poorly organized work area, lack of essential information, excessive red tape and paperwork, poorly planned procedures, failure to plan and implement priorities, poor skills in delegating, training and conceptualizing, procrastinating, poor scheduling, over-committing, attempting to do too much at once, and striving for perfection.

Creativity has its own force that often refuses to abide by logic, organization and discipline. However, one cannot deny that a successful career relies on the ability to manage time efficiently, in order to increase time for creativity. Time management tools must be employed if we want to decrease the stress that normal living can produce. You will decrease stress if you approach every task with calm and confidence, a positive attitude and clear idea of your priorities. Here are some more tips I find useful:

17 Time-Saving Tips

*Time is the measure of business,
as money is of wares.*
Francis Bacon

Be committed to the project at hand.
    The best way to become committed to a project is to become fully focused on the present. Organize the task and set aside sufficient time without any distractions. Rehearse the task mentally. Quiet the mind. Focus your attention. Take each step deliberately. Become totally absorbed in what you're doing, and a free-flowing momentum will transpire. You will get the job done faster and easier.

Manage your space.
    Create a separate work area. Use the spare room for an office or arrange a space in a corner of your studio or bedroom or even a closet. Keep materials organized and easy to locate. In this work area, you may place your phone, rolodex, appointment book, and a file cabinet to store your photographs, slide sheets, resume and business receipts. Keep this area free from visual and sound distractions that may interfere with your concentration. Eliminate clutter.

Keep a closed door to your private studio.
    This should be your sacred space, with times when you should let others know that you want to be left alone with your creativity. You should also provide time to brainstorm, daydream and to restore balance. Set limits on your social life and your family commitments.

Improve efficiency.

Once your career plans are incorporated into your daily routine, you will accomplish them with ease. Make and use lists, calendars and appointment books, manila folders, filing cabinets, index cards and other time-saving organizational methods. Alphabetize your files and organize your materials to help you locate them quickly. Buy and/or create such materials that are colorful, well designed and aesthetically appealing to you in order to make working with them a creative experience.

Set aside time each day and/or week to work on your career.

Just as it is important to find time to create the art, it is vital to find time to take care of business. Ideally, this should be a peak energy time when you have the ability to focus and concentrate on the details that can get easily lost along the way.

Be prepared.

Make tomorrow's plans and write your "to do" list the night before, so you don't waste time getting yourself focused in the morning. List all of the activities that need to get done and arrange them in order of urgency. Create promotional materials by the dozens. Have several sets of slides on file. Keep several copies of your current resume ready to go. Maintain your mailing list on the computer and keep it up to date.

Approach each project a step at a time.

One of the virtues of scheduling activities by time blocks is that it allows you to focus. But, are you setting important projects aside while waiting for that big block of time to be available? You'll discover that it will never arrive; it is better to use the five-minute strategy and tackle the project with small amounts of time on a regular basis. There are many time-savers that can be implemented, such as coupling projects together: For instance, open your mail while you talk on the phone.

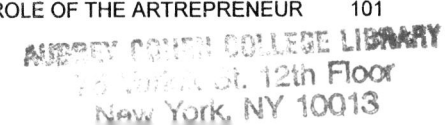

Exercise discipline.

One of the hardest aspects of a small business or home-based business is creating the discipline or motivation to work each day. It is so easy to get distracted and put off the essential tasks that need to get done. Keep your work place and hours separate from the rest of your responsibilities. Develop a to-do list everyday. Focus on your desire to complete the task and the rewards you will achieve. Find ways to make the process educational, entertaining and imaginative.

Take control.

Are you surprised that so much time disappears into thin air? Keep a time log for a week. List every project and activity and the time you spent, including chatting with friends on the phone, watching junk on TV, looking for papers that have not been filed away properly, and doing work that could be easily eliminated or delegated. This log will reveal how much time you actually waste.

Be aware of your actions: periodically, ask yourself whether the task you are doing is urgent or important. If neither, move on to something else that is.

Use modern technology.

Answering machines, fax machines, personal computers, copy machines and scanners are superb time-savers and necessary items for any business. They are also increasingly user-friendly and very affordable. Multi-purpose machines combine fax machines, phones and printers, which saves desk space and countless hours of manual labor. Put them to work for you.

Ask for help.

We all have different skills and talents and it is essential to learn to depend on others for assistance. All too often we are reluctant to ask for help and end up wasting time, becoming frustrated or making costly mistakes. Hire a specialist, such as a writer or publicist. You would be surprised how many outstanding freelancers are available for reasonable rates.

Delegate and share tasks.

Recruit high school or college interns to stretch canvases, arrange appointments, make deliveries, send faxes, make trips to the post office and type letters. Invite friends over for an envelope stuffing party accompanied by a good bottle of wine and classical music. Join an art organization in which fellow artists share career development activities.

Be adept at slowing time.

Be mindful of the way you pay attention to the small miracles. Reconnect with a sense of discovery and try to see events unfold through the eyes of a child, watching the first sunrise, or the miraculous way birds fly together in formations. Learn to meditate in your own way. This tip alone will reduce your stress level and help you become more productive.

Eliminate bad habits.

Dismiss all the irritations, the daily frustrations and predictable annoyances of your life once and for all! When you come across an integral problem, don't just fix it for now, get to the root of it and re-design your behavior. For example, if you find yourself spending too much time taking personal phone calls, either put a time limit on them or get an answering machine or Caller ID to monitor your incoming calls.

Avoid procrastination.

The pain of trying to pull off every detail at the last hour is much greater than finishing the tasks a little at a time over a period of months. Use a calendar in which to mark your deadlines. Keep an appointment book to help you stick to a schedule. If you have an exhibition six months from now, you should remove some of the tedious tasks that can be accomplished now, such as updating your resume and assembling your mailing list on your computer.

This is one of the major causes for failure. Some of the major reasons for procrastination are: fear of failure; fear of success; fear of change; fear of the unknown; fear of responsibilities; lack of motivation; lack of skill and lack of preparation. When you discover yourself procrastinating, try some self-analysis to get to the cause. Call your coach to help you get back on track.

Finish dreaded tasks first.

Most of us postpone a project we dislike, only to have it hang over our heads worrying about it, feeling guilty about not doing it, and finding excuses not to do it. If you just do it, you will feel a sense of relief to let you enjoy the rest of your time with more rewarding activities. Often, the dreaded tasks are not as undesirable as we thought and might bring positive results. For example, if you make the required phone call to the gallery to inquire about the status of your exhibition, you might get good news. Once you finish a dreaded task, reward yourself with a favorite activity or person.

Maintain good health.

In the battle against time and aging, you cannot ignore the correlation between good nutrition, mental and spiritual health, and the avoidance of disease. When your health is impaired, the future of your career will be threatened. Vitality is the reward for healthy living. Exercise regularly. Avoid the use of toxic artist materials, as well as toxic environments and relationships. You may frequently be tempted to work long and hard in your studio and neglect your nutritional needs. Have plenty of fresh fruits and vegetables and clean drinking water close at hand.

The circle is an irreducible geometric form which resonates universality, wholeness, completeness, integration, and absoluteness.

The Power of The Circle

Don't expect your career to proceed in an absolute linear direction. It may, instead, be viewed as an ever-changing composition of several overlapping circles such as dreams, creativity, fame, relationships and prosperity – much like the circles that spread out and overlap each other when you throw pebbles into a pond. One plus one will not always stack up to two, and you will be frustrated when you expect the outcome to equal your effort. You may excel in one area while at the same time lose momentum in another. That is to be expected.

If you pay attention, you will know instinctively which area will meet with the least resistance at any given time and you will find that opportunities will evolve if you follow that direction. I encourage you to be honest, knowledgeable, sensible and prepared, and to safeguard your destiny, but also to trust the flow and rhythm of your innate wisdom. Avoid stagnation. Keep the power of the circle expanding by casting many pebbles into the sea of possibilities.

Create a drawing that includes a configuration of overlapping circles, emanating from one central circle. The inner circle will be your purpose or dharma. The outside circles along the circumference will include all of the various venues, activities and choices that will help you fulfill your purpose. Attribute names to each circle, such as "relationships", "prosperity," etc. and see how they all interconnect. This exercise will help you to visualize the areas that are most important to you as those that need attention. Repeat the exercise often and compare them.

When nothing seems to help,
I go and look at a stonecutter
hammering away at his rock
perhaps a hundred times
without so much as a crack showing in it.
Yet at the hundred and first blow
it will split in two,
and I know it was not that blow that did it
but all that had gone before.
author unknown

Chapter 8

Create Your Master Plan! Master Your Destiny!

*He who controls others may be powerful,
but he who has mastered himself is mightier still.*
Lao Tsu

We all have a mission in life – one that guides us to a complete manifestation of our unique capabilities. I believe that there are guideposts very early in life that signal our destiny. It is apparent when you observe two children from the same family and each has a different set of preferences, aptitudes and behavioral responses to the same environmental factors. As I explained in the introduction of the book, the critical events that occurred in my childhood prepared me for my journey. At the time they occurred, I was frightened, shocked and confused, but when I look back now, the puzzle pieces fit together. There was a greater purpose for every experience – especially the most painful ones.

Your choice to be an artist is part of that purpose. But, the larger picture is your mission. What *kind* of artist do you want to be? What do you want to *do* with your art? What do you want to be known for? Your art can serve as a catalyst if your mission is to participate in social change. It can provide solace for broken hearts if your mission is to heal. It can be stimuli for important dialogue among different people from around the globe if your mission is to unite. In identifying your mission, examine the events in your life in which you reacted most strongly. They will help you identify your essence.

Know thyself.
Socrates

Your mission is more than your role, as parent, teacher, artist or writer. It is who you were before you assumed these roles, and who you will continue to be when the roles change throughout your life. If you define yourself by your role you will be unfulfilled and always searching for more.

Ideally, your job should align with your mission. My friend Maggie has a well-paid position in a technological field. When she started in the profession several years ago it challenged her and she enjoyed a fruitful relationship with her co-workers. Last year she began to experience enormous stress and anxiety produced by office politics, corporate downsizing and co-workers' bickering. She was feeling a sense of powerlessness.

Maggie lost the positive reasons that led her to this profession. No longer feeling rewarded, she began to examine her needs for self-discovery and renewal. Once she viewed the larger picture she realized that she is much more than her job and she had the power to make some fundamental changes. She incorporated more creativity and self-expression into her life which has made her feel more complete and fulfilled. Now that she has empowered herself she is seeking another career direction that is more compatible with her mission and skills.

If you continue to ignore the importance of realizing your dreams, don't be surprised if you often feel as though you're lost at sea without a compass. Having a vision on the horizon begins with an honest introspection of your aspirations. If you continuously stay in tune with your life's purpose, you will always carry a sense of inner harmony and balance; your soul will continue to grow with each new revelation, and with the feeling of peace and joy. You will be able to remove insurmountable obstacles with a feather.

Examine your personal values and order of priorities. Once you've established what's truly important, you can avoid being plagued by conflicting choices that offer different sets of values. For example, if you want to express hope for universal harmony and need to travel worldwide to embrace different cultures, you will be unhappy if you accept a highly paid art teaching job in a small town. You will feel stifled if you are immobile.

Mandela's mission was to end apartheid; Mother Teresa's mission was to offer solace to the sick and end human suffering. Your mission is something you know at the core of your being is your strong passion. As soon as you establish your mission, you can proceed to prepare your goals. If you reverse the order, you may find yourself very preoccupied with "to-do" lists without making a rewarding contribution to yourself or others.

If you were to write your eulogy, what would it say? How are you going to be remembered? What values did you express? How did you change lives? All great journeys begin with a desired destination. Embrace those elusive dreams that often seem out of reach, and weave them into your every day habits to make them tangible. What action could you take right *Now!* that would set your dream in motion? Create your master plan. Master your destiny!

Nothing happens unless first a dream.
Carl Sandburg

Your Career Goals

As an artist career advisor, I have learned that at the root of many career problems lies uncertainty about the future and a feeling of powerlessness. Part of my role as an advisor is to help artists clarify their goals and identify the problems that are standing in their way. So, before the consultation begins, I ask the artist to provide, along with their presentation materials, a short list of their career objectives. I usually ask, "Where do you want to be one or two years from now? What do you want to gain from this consultation?" From the answers I receive I am able to tune into the artist's values, priorities and outlook. The exercise also enables them to take charge of their career direction and focus on the outcome. By examining the full picture – the artist's art work, career history and objectives – I can begin to offer a specific range of appropriate and realistic strategies, leads and resources. I have also applied the routine of questioning in my group workshops. Artists are encouraged to define and clarify their goals. They leave the workshop with specific strategies. They make a commitment to take active steps in the pursuit of these goals and bring the results back to the next workshop. Both negative and positive results are discussed, specific problems are solved, and they move to the next step.

It is important to write long-term and short-term goals in order of priority. Be specific. It is not sufficient to say: "I want fame and fortune." What is your precise definition of fame that would make you happy? At what cost? How long are you willing to wait? Are your goals compatible? Acknowledge and incorporate your individual personality and needs and what is essential for you to be happy and fulfilled. Examine your energy levels and set realistic and reasonable time frames in accordance. Make sure your goal comes from your heart and not from your head. Be sure your goal is what you truly want and not what somebody else thinks you should be doing. Temporarily disassociate yourself from your peers; avoid confusing the values and goals of those in your sphere of influence with your own.

> *We act as though comfort and luxury were the chief requirements of life, when all that we need to make us happy is something to be enthusiastic about.*
> Charles Kingsley

Ponder the words of Dr. Robert Schuller: "What would you attempt to do if you knew you could not fail?" Would you quit your job and become a full-time artist? Would you move to Europe and sculpt huge pieces in marble? Would you open a gallery? Would you bring creative workshops to hospices?

Once you have envisioned your dream as your goal, begin forging your way through the wilderness to your destination. Foresee any barriers and obstacle courses before they appear. Have alternative plans ready. Take the path of least resistance – the easiest, most direct, and safest route. Choose a combination of activities and priorities that feel right.

Determine where the hurdles are by asking: What is stopping me from having my goals met? How will achieving my goal affect other areas in my life? What are the positive and negative consequences of reaching my aspirations? What resources do I already have, and what additional resources do I need in order to accomplish my goals? Be willing to change self-sabotaging habits that lead you off your course.

A goal is a dream with deadlines.

Take action. Once you know where you want to go and have a path designed to get there, start *now*! Don't let anything stand in your way. When Susan made the commitment to finish seven paintings to show to a prospective dealer, she initially panicked and, then asked me to help her with a plan. She cleared her schedule of everything non-essential. She told her friends she wouldn't be available for recreation. She prepared a few meals for her family and put them in the freezer, and supplied them menus from take-out restaurants. She turned on her answering machine and turned off the volume. She spent eight hours a day in her studio with the door closed, until she finished the paintings. She refused to allow any distractions to deter her, and she exited her studio victoriously!

It is important to give your goals a voice. Talk about them with enthusiasm and confidence with those who sincerely want you to attain them. Knowing that family, friends, business partners or the entire world is cheering for us, counting on us and supporting us is critically important. Recruit one artist or a group of artists and encourage each other to stay on track, especially during difficult setbacks. Do you know anyone who does *not* want you to succeed? Keep them away from you.

You should spend at least five minutes alone in the beginning of each day quietly and deliberately, focusing on the course of your life as an artist. Make a list of activities that you need to perform, in priority order. After your list is the way you want it, make the commitment to proceed. Take immediate action. Make the phone call, write the letter, plant the seed. When you accomplish the activities, cross them off the list with a big red marker!

Create new goal plans periodically, and set higher ones with each triumph. Be flexible. When one plan doesn't work, try another!

Affluence means "to flow in abundance."
Let prosperity flow through you.

Your Financial Goals

Professional power increases with financial security. The first step to obtaining financial prosperity is deciding the amount of money you require to live the kind of lifestyle you desire and how much money you need to operate your business. You also need to take a look at your cash flow, which is discussed in a previous section of this book.

It is essential to have a financial goal if you want to grow your business. Is your business plan prepared? Have you written down the actual dollar amount you want to earn in order to establish security as a full-time artist? Are you satisfied with last year's income? What steps will you take to improve your financial situation next year? At the same time, remember to keep things in perspective: Are you merely more wealthy this year or are you richer in character? What have you learned from the goals you did not reach?

List your financial goal for the coming year. Decide how many works of art you will need to sell in order to reach that goal. If your annual goal is $50,000 sales of your artwork, and your average selling price is $500, you will need about 100 sales. In order to reach those prospects, you will need to invest time and money, such as in exhibition expenses, direct mail, printing and art supplies.

If your work is painstakingly detailed and it can compete among the best, enter as many of the prize-winning competitions and, by winning the prizes, it boost your value as well as build recognition and exposure of your works of art. Your strategy to try to sell the works for what they are worth in time and effort will be excruciatingly difficult, especially if you are new. Better to build up a record of prizes and accolades and gain financial support through other means, until you can demand the right price.

If you create sculpture or paintings that require extensive work and can only complete one or two each year, you need a different set of financial goals than a prolific artist who turns out six paintings a week.

Are you willing to make some short-term sacrifices and compromises in order to reach your long-term goals? Is the fact that you may be too idealistic, fearful or inflexible preventing you from realizing your desired goals?

"Use Green Power" Seize Your Potential for Wealth

The subject of finances is often a difficult subject to discuss with an artist. Money is a very sensitive issue and carries a hefty weight of emotional baggage. Take, for example, an artist who is financially dependent upon her or his spouse. Questions about need, self-worth and self-sufficiency can interfere with an artist's career if not addressed properly and if solutions are not found.

Catharine came to me for a consultation at the end of the calendar year. Her financial situation was definitely a priority of concern; she and her husband had recently analyzed her business as an artist. She hadn't sold any work in the previous year. Her husband tried to reassure her by saying he would try – but could not promise – to allocate $1,500 toward her career in the next year.

We could have spent her consultation time solving Catharine's immediate challenge of working within the limitations of $1,500. However, I chose to help her make a more positive change in her life of much greater magnitude. We began to examine and discuss her attitude about her career, her relationship with money and the value she placed on her art. She realized that it was time to change the pattern and take steps to empower herself. In her mind, she had limited herself to dependency upon her husband and, furthermore, to accept receiving no more than the $1,500. However, if we focused on that limitation, she would forever repeat this pattern of needing her husband's resources to invest in her career.

First, we took out Catharine's presentation materials and discussed them as her "sales force." How were they serving to attract sales? What did they say about the value of her work and herself as an artist? They needed to be improved. We reconstructed a biography that emphasized her career achievements and minimized her career weaknesses.

I also advised her to join more professional organizations in which to exhibit her work; the arts organizations she belonged to had lower artistic standards than she deserved. I encouraged her to apply for juried exhibitions jurored by museum curators. If she were accepted, in the year ahead she would achieve better credentials, in addition to securing more visibility for her work and increasing her potential for sales.

Next, I encouraged Catharine to apply herself to becoming more verbal about her work. There was nothing about her art work that would lead anyone to believe that they were not salable. However, Catharine was quite secretive about her work. I encouraged her to communicate to everyone, including friends, relatives, and associates, that her art was available for sale. We discussed her need to develop relationships with corporate art consultants and private art dealers. I gave her a list of leads and sample brochures.

We then discussed Catharine's prices. She showed me a neatly, typewritten list of thirty works available for sale. For a limited track record, I thought they were marked too high. We adjusted the prices by fifteen percent. In her situation, it would be better to build a sales history and customer base. That way as she moved the thirty works from her inventory she would have room for future works. Later on, I explained, as she amassed more sales, she could increase her prices.

My next question startled Catharine, as I pointed to her new price list: "What if you were to look at this inventory of art work as money waiting to be collected? That would be a total of $15,000. How long it will take depends on you and how much effort you apply." That question marked the turning point in the consultation. It showed her the wealth of potential that was in her grasp, and it had the power to make a positive impact on her attitude and, ultimately, her entire career.

From that moment on, a radical change in Catharine's posture and self-esteem occurred. We began forming strategies to help her reach that $15,000 mark. We also discussed ways to perceive her artwork as a useful instrument that could be bartered for framing, promotion, equipment, art workshops and printing – a valuable vehicle that would increase her income and enhance her creative freedom. She began to see money as "Green Power" that had the capacity to fuel her dreams into bringing tangible results.

Catharine is not the only individual who had to learn how to develop a healthy relationship with money. Many artists and other professionals have no idea whether or not they are making any money, or where their profits or customers come from, and whether the numbers are going up or down. They have no control over it. Every aspect of your business is either making money or costing you money. If it's costing you money, you have to make changes, or you will quickly find defeat. (Remember the earlier section on "Cash Flow"?)

The sooner you get comfortable with money and build a productive relationship with it, you will gain the power to access it and grow it. If you want to avoid business failure, you have to pay attention to the numbers. When you learn how to manage the process of building assets, you will no longer see it as intimidating or boring; it will become an exhilarating experience to build your financial power.

> *Picture yourself vividly as winning*
> *and that alone will contribute immeasurably to success.*
> *Great living starts with a picture,*
> *held in your imagination, of what you would like to be.*
> Dr. Harry Emerson Fosdick

Visualize Your Goals

As a visual artist, you have keen visual perception and are most stimulated by what you see. Use that skill to activate the power of visualization in association to where you want to be, with whom you want to be, and the kind of life style you will have.

Ask yourself: How will I benefit from achieving my goal? Being clear and specific about the benefits that will come from completing your goals is a powerful stimulus.

Before your exhibition, visualize a large number of guests at your opening reception showing appreciation for your work with open check books in hand.

Look for pictures of artists' studios, travel spots, houses, galleries, apparel and other images that attract you, and make them your goals.

Cut out magazine ads from galleries where you want your work shown, and paste an image of your work inside the ad.

Surround yourself with positive affirmations, talented people, great books, posters and collages describing your goals in rich, vivid pictures. Place positive images where you can see them everyday. Pin them to your studio wall next to your certificate of awards and letters of acceptances as a reminder of your past achievements and your future possibilities.

These activities will clarify your goals and will offer tangible rewards that will motivate you to take action in order to attain them.

> *Experience is not what happens to a man,*
> *it is what a man does with what happens to him.*
> Aldous Huxley

Enjoy the Process

Once you plan your strategies, be patient and consistent in your efforts, and don't expect immediate results. Enjoy the journey. Exercise discipline and adhere to deadlines. Develop a schedule and routine that works for you. Break down larger goals into daily activities. Make lists of tasks to be done, cross them off with a thick, colored marker, and reward yourself with time to play! And remember, your life is more than setting and attaining goals. The rewards are derived from the kind of person you grow into during your pursuit and at the final outcome.

Associate positive feelings and rewards with the activities you will be performing on your way to reach your goals. If you are a teacher focus on the gratification that you will receive from sharing your knowledge with others who need and desire it, and how it will increase your own education and spiritual growth. If you decide to print your first catalog, concentrate on how it will enhance your self-esteem, and offer something of beauty to individuals who admire your work and countless more who will become acquainted with it. If your goal is to produce limited edition prints, think about how making your art more accessible to a larger market will increase your exposure and profits. When you associate positive feelings such as these you will augment the significance of your efforts, boost your morale, and speed the process that will lead you to your desired goals.

*Our doubts are traitors, and make us lose
the good we oft might win, by fearing to attempt.*
William Shakespeare

The difference between the successful person who achieves his goals and others who do not, is not the amount of physical prowess, nor the accumulation of financial wealth, nor level of education, but the intensity of desire and commitment to make it happen.

Charles Darwin said: "It is not the strongest of the species that survive, nor the most intelligent, but the one most responsive to change." Julia Soul said: "If you are never scared, embarrassed or hurt, it means you never take chances." If the fear of failure is preventing you from making a sincere effort, remember one thing all successful people have in common is that they have all tried and failed many times along the road to success.

Shoot for the moon.
Even if you miss it you will land among the stars.
Les Brown

It is one thing to strive for high goals – to shoot for the stars – as long as you are content to enjoy the view from the clouds and the branches of the trees. Be careful if you define success as achieving perfection, an impossible dream; it is far better to aim toward attaining excellence – a tangible reality. In your journey to reach the pinnacle of success, avoid becoming so overly obsessed with the outcome that you reprimand and torment yourself every time you stumble and stub your toe.

During the process of creating your art, don't focus on wanting the sale or adulation. Use the process as an opportunity to explore your emotions, values and fears, and allow them to become a growth experience – to deepen your relationship with yourself. Remember, there is great value in creating art even if it turns out not to your liking, you can savor the process of exploring a new idea, technique or perspective. Perfectionism is a self-sabotaging activity that invites the critic and the judge to enter your sacred realm and sit on each of your shoulders, dictating your every move. When you hear their voices, you must ignore them, for they will argue incessantly and drive you mad. Toss them off your shoulders, laugh at them, as a child would, and frolic in the garden of discovery and spontaneity.

If by being a perfectionist is preventing you from finishing a work of art, you must learn when it is time to stop or you may need assistance or take a break for a while. Accept the fact that a work of art is never really "finished," nor does it need to be in order to serve its purpose. The great masters have taught us that there is more than one way to approach a subject. Monet's series of haystacks and ponds is a good example of painting repeated views of the same subject, each one "perfect" in their own right.

Some goals are so large or so far off that they are really just dreams or fantasies. A useful goal is one that you can work on today.

> *Life's a banquet, and most poor suckers*
> *are starving to death.*
> Auntie Mame

Celebrate!

We spend so much time in states of frustration, need, impatience and sacrifice, and not enough time in celebration. No wonder we often drag ourselves around, feeling pulled down from the weight of the world. We would all feel much lighter if we remembered to rejoice frequently in our accomplishments and savor every morsel of our success!

The next time you finish a work of art, take time out to give yourself a standing ovation! When you receive a phone call with an invitation to have an exhibition after you hang up the phone, jump for joy, do the jig, roar with laughter, grin from ear to ear, until your jaws ache. For every achievement, buy yourself a special present. Open a bottle of Champagne. Celebrate!

Ann called me several times during the process of curating a show. She complained about the friction among the artists, trying to get everyone to agree, hurt egos, late payments, framing, photography and installation woes. Although it was very serious to her, most of her grievances were minor, easily corrected, and often exaggerated. Unfortunately, the attention she was giving to the "small stuff" was interrupting her flow of creativity and productivity. One day I stopped her in the middle of the sentence and said: "Ann, celebrate! You should be proud of yourself for having curated an exhibition, for having created new work and for bringing a creative concept to fruition! You should be looking forward to the opening reception!" She paused, then laughed! I suddenly got her to see the larger picture. She had accomplished her goal and had forgotten to rejoice. Once she realized that, the tone of her voice immediately changed, and I could tell she was smiling.

Be aware of the occasions when you should be patting yourself on the back instead of focusing on the negative. Take the time to extend those moments when you get a pang of pride – whether you receive an award or finish a commission, or an important person returns your call. Thank yourself for attaining your goals and show gratitude to others in your life for their support. Celebrate!

*The ideal artist is he who knows everything,
feels everything, experiences everything,
and retains his experience in a spirit of wonder
and feeds upon it with creative lust.
He is therefore best able to select and order the
components best suited to fulfill any given desire.
The ideal artist is the superman.
He uses every possible power, spirit, emotion –
conscious or unconscious – to arrive at his ends.*
George Bellows

Your Career Goal: An Exercise

<u>Sample Goal:</u> Produce a catalog of my work

Action list:
1. Select the paintings that should go into the catalog.
2. Call the photographer to arrange an appointment.
3. Call the art magazine for a referral of a writer for the catalog.
4. Look in my "Idea File" for sample catalogs.
5. Get quotes from printers.

<u>Sample Goal:</u> Obtain a new studio to create larger sculpture

Action list:
1. Determine my budget.
2. Calculate my space requirements.
3. Post notices on bulletin boards in art supply stores.
4. Call artist organizations and newsletters for leads.
5. Apply for a workspace grant.

Your Goal: _____

Action list:
1. _____
2. _____
3. _____
4. _____
5. _____

Your Financial Goal: An Exercise

Along with a business plan your action list might include:
1. Take a course in financial planning.
2. Leave the gallery that hasn't sold any work in 2 years.
3. Increase income from selling limited edition prints or smaller works in addition to large pieces.
4. Create a direct mail piece and reach a target market.
5. Raise my prices by 15%.

There may be many other different avenues you can choose that will augment your income. For example, how many students would you need and how much would you need to charge if you began giving lectures and/or classes in your studio? How many smaller works can you create to reach more buyers and what can you charge for these small pieces? And how would you go about accomplishing these challenges? Visualize yourself as already having earned your financial goal. Visualize yourself investing and spending your money once you've earned it. Make a list of the art supplies, products, advertising, trips, and other investments you will make.

Your Financial Goal $_____
Deadline:_____

Action list:
1. _____
2. _____
3. _____
4. _____
5. _____

Chapter 9

Competitions
Are they Worth the Gamble?

*At last I could work
with complete independence
without concerning myself
with the eventual judgment of a jury...
I began to live.*
Mary Cassatt
(Her statement after the Salon rejected her painting)

Juried competitions/exhibitions are viewed by many artists, not only as opportunities to have their work juried by respected professionals for career advancement, but as ways to increase exposure, sales and awards. If they take place in noted museums and art councils they are considered more prestigious than commercial galleries. For many artists, who have yet to find gallery representation, competitions serve as the only venues for exposure. Many dealers seek new talent in such alternative spaces. Artists who are awarded juried museum and gallery exhibitions may gain collectors' interest and receive critical acclaim. Competitions that produce catalogues, present purchase and cash awards, and other prizes are difficult to resist. For these reasons many artists who previously considered competitions unfair and/or unnecessary have reconsidered their merits. However, as appealing as juried shows may be, even the best competitions reward only the few.

A Toss of the Dice

Many artists are adamantly opposed to juried competitions that charge fees to have their work juried. Several artists I have interviewed believe competitive exhibitions are a waste of time and money. To them, it is a matter of luck or connections, not skill, that determines the outcome. The identical work of art entered in the same competition may win one year and get rejected the next. The process is far from an exact science. Although jurors try to be objective and fair-minded, everyone is influenced by subjective decision-making. It helps to learn about the tastes of the jurors before submitting work. Artists should attend the exhibitions or peruse the catalogues to learn about the sponsors' and judges' standards, in order to determine whether the show is worth pursuing the following year.

American Artist magazine is one of the most comprehensive sources for competition listings. According to its Editor-in-Chief M. Stephen Doherty: "Competitions offer some good news and some bad news. The good news is, ultimately, the competitions are based on quality alone. Artists who live in Belgium and South Africa are offered an equal opportunity to receive recognition with artists who live in major cities in the United States. However, each year there are tougher competitors. The number of entries increase." He added: "Often the ultimate decisions by the judges are somewhat arbitrary and several hundred artists may have to be thrown out simply because there is no space."

Big-Name Jurors

Although the objective is to win, many artists feel certain competitions are worth entering, even if they don't win, because they know their entries will be viewed by esteemed art professionals. Gallery 84, a former New York City cooperative gallery, attracted nearly 1,000 entries and 4,000 slides to its 1994 Annual Competition. Gallery Director Joe Bascom attributed the overwhelming response to the presence of juror Donald Kuspit, a prominent art critic, and the gallery's prestigious Fifty-Seventh Street location. The competition selected only twenty five winners – about 2-1/2% of the entries. These figures are representative of most major city exhibitions judged by major critics and museum curators. The winners of competitions of this caliber may believe that their work ranks among the best of the best. High tolerance to rejection is required when entering competitions. Artists should rely on more events in their careers than competitions as monitors of the value of their work, or they will be setting themselves up for disappointment.

Competitions as Fair Game

Competitions reflect global changes and keep pace with today's political and social climate and pressure. Today, competitions are as varied as the styles and media chosen by artists. Many competitions specifically call for female artists, physically challenged artists, young artists, senior artists, and Asian-American artists, to name a few.

Juried exhibitions in non-profit venues offer what many commercial galleries do not – a level playing field. Artists are judged on the merit of their work, not by their resumes or monetary value. They offer hope to minority artists, young artists starting out, and more mature artists who may be restarting their careers. New York Artists Equity Association held a competition open to all members. It was juried by Geno Rodriguez, Director of the Alternative Museum, in NYC. It attracted 800 artists from around the country: 55% of the entrants were women. Unaware of the gender of any of the entrants, Rodriguez selected 29 artists, of which 21 were women. Several years ago, Pernod (producer of the French aperitif), held an open competition, with four judges from New York art community, including Robert Storr, curator of Contemporary Painting and Sculpture at the Museum of Modern Art, and art critic Carlo McCormick. The rules specifically stated: "Open to any artist who has not had a one-person show at an "established" or "professional gallery." There was no entry fee. The first-place winner received $5,000 and a group exhibition in a SoHo, New York gallery, with nine additional winners. More than 2,300 works of art were entered by 300 artists. This approach makes businesses sense. Pernod generated positive publicity for their products. It is a practice that should be followed by more companies that want to gain exposure to an art audience.

The Financial Picture

The average entry fee for juried competitions is $25. For many non-profit organizations and artist-run galleries, these calls for artists help to offset annual expenses. The entry fees have to cover the costs for advertising the competitions, jurors' fees, printing and mailing of prospectuses, exhibition reception costs, printing of the exhibition invitations, catalogs, staff salaries, and advertising for the exhibition. Jurors' fees can run up to a few thousand dollars for some highly esteemed museum curators. However, some prominent jurors volunteer their services for the experience of viewing the entries. Others are compensated with a work of art. And, other lesser-known jurors agree to judge in exchange for the publicity and professional credentials they gain.

Artists Beware

For some opportunists, competitions serve as quick and easy profits. Their method is to promise a lot and deliver little. You may recall the New England Fine Art Institute's "State of the Art '93" juried competition. An estimated number of 2,600 artists paid a minimum of $25 to enter, and an additional $49 fee to have their work hung, when selected. It was discovered by the artists who attended the exhibition that many of the art works remained in their crates and were never exhibited. The "Institute" was revealed to be, in fact, a small, temporary, rented office space. Numerous complaints were made to the Complaint Division of the Eastern Massachusetts Better Business Bureau and to George K. Weber, Assistant Attorney General, Commonwealth of Massachusetts.

Warning Signs

It is important for artists to make formal complaints when events like this occur, but it is more important to avoid them. There are many signs to took for when judging the quality of a competition. Here are some obvious warnings:

• The prospectus or entry form is unprofessionally written and/or poorly printed.

• No telephone number is listed.

- A post office box is supplied for an unknown institution.
- The names of the jurors are not stated.
- The jurors are professionally unqualified.
- The organizers cannot supply adequate, detailed information about previous competition winners and cash prizes.
- The sponsor holds continuous competitions throughout the year.
- In addition to the entry fees, there are hanging charges or exhibition-related expenses.

Proceed with Caution

Even if the material appears to look professional, you should be prepared to research the organization and ask for references. If the sponsor is unknown, check the Better Business Bureau, Chamber of Commerce, and regional and national art organizations. If the sponsor claims to be a foundation, check The Foundation Center, in NYC. *(See Appendix 2.)* If it is the organizer's first attempt, check them thoroughly. Share your suspicions and information with other artists, professional art organizations and art publications that expose fraudulent practices, such as *Art Calendar* and *Success Now! For Artists*. These publications also list reputable competitions in museums, galleries and other venues. Today, there are growing numbers of websites that offer listings, such as the Art Deadlines List. *(See Appendix 4).*

How to be Competitive

If the competition passes the legitimacy test and you are ready to take the plunge, you should follow some basic guidelines. If you are being juried by slides, make sure they are of the best quality available. Don't submit slides that are out of focus, with scratches, glare, or distracting objects. Use silver or black masking tape when required. View the slides in a projector before submitting them to the jurors. Make sure the slide slips into the plastic sleeve easily and is not warped. Label your slides correctly, according to the specifications outlined on the prospectus. Type the information on adhesive labels (that will not fall off when subjected to the heat of the projector), or use non-smearing ink. Use plastic sleeves; don't throw the slides loosely into an envelope. Mail the slides with protective padding. Follow every instruction in the prospectus. Unless another size is requested enclose a business-sized (4 1/8" x 9-1/2") self-addressed, postage-paid envelope with the proper amount of postage, for the return of your slides.

When selecting slides, remember that in most situations your work has less than one minute to make an impact. One gallery reported a major art critic took only two hours to view a few hundred slides. Another one in a New York gallery took less than an eight-hour day to view 1,000 slides.

I have juried several dozen competitions of all types and sizes over the years. Most judges I have known, like myself, seek technical prowess as well as innovation. So, when making your selection, be objective, and ask: Are you entering your best works or are there obvious technical flaws? Are you submitting a lackluster still life that will blend in with the hundreds of other still life entries or is your piece more dramatic, innovative or risk-taking? Does your work evoke a strong reaction? Does the composition impact the viewer and retain their attention?

If the competition requires judging from original works of art, pay attention to proper matting, framing, and packaging.

It is not the critic who counts:
not the man who points out
how the strong man stumbled
or where the doer of deeds
could have done better.
The credit belongs to the man
who is actually in the arena,
whose face is marred
with dust, sweat and blood;
who strives valiantly;
who errs and comes up short again;
who knows with great enthusiasm,
the great devotion;
who spends himself in a worthy cause;
who, at best, knows the triumph
of high achievement,
and at worst,
at least fails while daring greatly.
Theodore Roosevelt

Chapter 10

Rejection
It's All a Matter of Perspective

I was taught that the way of progress
is neither swift nor easy.
Marie Curie

As you take strides to improve your professional life, rejection will tap on your door periodically as a test of your convictions. Instead of running for cover, invite it in to be a teacher. Examine your reactions to this demon, and you'll find clues for possible changes to avoid the magnitude of its effects in the future. Refuse to let it oppress you. Build a beautiful fortress around yourself, constructed with a positive attitude, confidence and constructive plans of action.

Rejection as a Catalyst

Look at rejection as if it were a bridge to another place – a growth experience. Your destiny can be devastation or enlightenment – the choice is yours. Rejection can serve as a powerful stimulus to creative productivity. As an artist you have the advantage of being able to express your pain through your eyes and the process can be a miraculous healer. Seize the feeling and turn the experience of rejection into a work of art. It may be among the most satisfying works you have ever created because the emotions are still fresh and within your grasp. Who knows what buried treasures you will discover once you dig below the surface and face the demons?

During a very painful period in her life – after learning about her husband's infidelity – Beverly was propelled into creating a patchwork quilt. Each patch that she made expressed a different range of emotions that she experienced through the process of her divorce. It took several months, but with each stitch her rage, resentment and hatred came pouring out. The project liberated her from the pain probably a lot quicker than if she had gone to a therapist or chosen to prolong her suffering through resentment and bitterness by doing nothing. Afterward, she sold the quilt – it became an act that finalized the process of letting go of the pain and anger. Released from the suffering, and more empowered than ever before, she could move on with her life.

Surely, a rejection by a gallery, grant-giver or critic pales in comparison to betrayal or divorce. But, you can take Beverly's lead and recognize the importance of separating yourself from the pain and, thereby, refusing to be a victim. Get through your fears with the healing power of creativity and walk down the path where faith can be restored.

The Importance of Objectivity

When you experience the pain of rejection examine your feelings, linking them to patterns in the past. Transform them into a language that is healing and provides nourishment. After you experience rejection, step back and watch the events unravel objectively, as though you were watching a movie about someone else. A few questions may reveal helpful answers for improvement: At what point did the situation go sour? The artwork you presented, did it reflect your best work? In your personal interview, was your attitude enthusiastic and confident, or defensive and self-conscious? Did you make a sincere effort with your mailing and send out more than a handful of proposals? Does your exhibition history match those of the other artists who are vying for the same gallery as you? Are the jurors in the competition partial to another style? Were there politics involved? Did you rely on someone else to carry through your responsibilities? These are a few examples of causes that can lead to rejection. If the reason is obvious, you can avoid repeating the experience. With some research and awareness of the circumstances, you can take corrective action and avoid future disappointments.

In many situations, you may never know the reason why your work was rejected. If so, don't waste your energy trying to analyze something you may never understand. There are many uncontrollable factors that have nothing to do with you or the quality of your work.

Rejection is frequently merely the result of an opinion of one or more individuals. In the final analysis, the only evaluation that should be of real value to you should be your own. Don't search for others to validate your work.

Dollars and Sense

When a dealer rejects your work, there is a very good reason not to take it personally. There countless reasons behind their decisions and they may have nothing to do with the merit of the work itself. First of all, the business of dealing in art is a business. The dealer must consider whether the gallery has the right clientele for your work. There might not be room at this time for another artist. They may be going through partnership changes. They may prefer to wait and watch you evolve before taking the plunge. Do not expect every dealer to comprehend the heart, soul, feelings and ideas that went into your work. The heart and the bank account may often seem to be very far apart from each other.

Corinne Shane is President of InvestinArt, an art consulting business in New York City, whose clients consist of corporations. When she assisted me in jurying the 1997 Cover Art Competition for *Manhattan Arts International* magazine, in response to many of the submissions, she said: "I love the work, but it is not suitable for my corporate clients." If she were selling to private individuals, her choices would fit a different criteria. And, she will admit, as would most art buyers about art, that it is a very subjective matter.

If you place a dozen art critics, collectors and art dealers in a room together with a wide variety of art work, chances are they will not agree on which works are the best and the worst. And, they are likely to change their minds during and after the process of discussion. I have frequently heard from artists that they submitted their work to one gallery, and it was rejected, however, the same work won a top award in a competition. History has proven time and again that the judgments of "experts" have not only varied, but changed over a period of time. Make your own decision about what has value.

Remember, genuine interest in Vincent van Gogh's came after his death. Rauschenberg's first show at Leo Castelli Gallery barely got off the ground. Jean Dubuffet didn't have his first exhibition until he reached the ripe age of 43. The Whitney Biennials have become the show many critics love to hate. For several years people have muttered that painting is dead, yet we know it is far from its demise. Hundreds of similar facts and opinions are chronicled in great detail in many history books. You don't have to look far to find proof that rejection should not deter you from your career course.

> *"Don't judge each day by the harvest you reap, but by the seeds you sow."*
> Robert Louis Stevenson

If you're not receiving as many acceptances as you would like, examine the methods you are currently using. Review your five-year plan; it may need some changes. Does it still fit your needs? Does it support the changes in the economy? Do you need to search for new alternatives? What useful tactics of successful role models can you apply?

If you feel defeated by rejections when approaching dealers with your work, find a friend or a relative who will present your materials on your behalf. Most dealers don't care if the artist introduces his or her work, or if a representative does, but rather, if the type of work is appropriate for their gallery. If the work is found to be of interest, the dealer will arrange to see the work in person.

Increase your options and increase your odds. A good way to minimize rejection is through diversification. You certainly wouldn't put your entire life's savings into one stock fund and you shouldn't put all of your faith into one individual or outlet. Develop a broad and healthy marketing plan that includes several galleries, competitions, private dealers and grants – on a regional, national and international level. Sell multiples in addition to your originals. Vary the sizes and prices of your work.

Develop a system that has a steady momentum and routine. Keep your eyes and ears open for new galleries, changes in administration, and burgeoning services and opportunities offered through arts organizations.

Diversification, combined with a productive routine, will not only increase your potential for success, it will cushion rejection when it comes: You will be too busy to allow rejection to paralyze you.

> *Results!*
> *I have gotten thousands of results.*
> *I know several thousand things that won't work.*
> Thomas A. Edison

Instead of brooding over sluggish sales, look to the future and what you will achieve. Calculate the number of attempts you have to make before you finally sell a work of art or acquire a commission. Divide the selling price by that number. Every time you receive a rejection, say to yourself, "I just made 'X' amount of money, and am 'X' prospects closer to meeting the buyer."

Every time you receive a rejection notice, balance the scales by sending out more proposals and making more phone calls, and thereby increasing your chances of receiving positive feedback.

Don't Burn Your Bridges

In the face of rejection, be as gracious as possible, keep your dignity intact, and don't burn any bridges. If one gallery rejects your work this year, it does not necessarily mean that the door is closed forever. If you think your work is appropriate for them, try again later. Many dealers observe new artists over several years before making a commitment. Also, many events may affect their attitude later, such as the director may get fired, their finances may improve, or the quantity and styles of their artists may shift. I have known artists to be rejected by the directors of the galleries only to be later contacted by the assistant directors who opened their *own* galleries. Keep the lines of communication open.

> *The pessimist sees the difficulty in every opportunity.*
> *The optimist, the opportunity in every difficulty.*
> Winston Churchill

Len, a positive and assertive artist, announced at one of my "Success Now!" workshops that he submitted materials to a New York gallery. He thought the gallery was the right one for his work, however, to his dismay, his slides were returned by the owner with a polite rejection letter. It stated that, although she liked his work, she was not currently looking for new artists.

Many artists in this situation might have lost hope and become bitter and depressed, but Len's confidence in his work, and his knowledge of the gallery system kept his momentum going. A few weeks later when he entered his slides into a national competition, judged by Klaus Kertess, out of a few hundred entries, he was selected with nine other artists. He promptly informed the aforementioned dealer of his upcoming exhibition in a cover letter, which he enclosed with the same slides he originally submitted to her.

Within two weeks, he received a call from her and an invitation to be included in a group exhibition.

Was it coincidence? Did the dealer change her mind after learning about the "stamp of approval" given by Klaus Kertess? I don't know. But, I do know that if Len hadn't entered the competition and had not resubmitted his work to the gallery, he might never had been invited to show in that group exhibition. The lesson here is never give up!

As tempting as it might be, you do not want to burn all of your rejection letters, but rather, file them with your business receipts, according to tax advisors. They help prove to the IRS that you are making every attempt to sell your work and that you are not a hobbyist. Then, if you take a loss on Schedule C, you have legitimate proof that you are engaging in professional activities.

Success is simply a matter of luck.
Ask any failure.
Earl Wilson

Luck is When Preparation Meets Opportunity

Luck, you may say, plays a role. Innate talent, intelligence and economic background are also helpful, but the saying: "It takes fifteen years of hard work to become an overnight success" suggests that persistence is the most important factor.

Susan is a sculptor who was continuously turned down by New York galleries until a leading New York dealer saw one of her pieces in a doctor's office and asked her to join the gallery.

Thomas is a painter who decided to try a different route and arranged an exhibition of his work in a bank, where the wife of a major software company owner saw it and purchased one of his works for her house.

Jane, a watercolor artist, boarded a plane, opened her sketch pad and soon realized she was sitting next to a very curious art collector.

Luis placed his hanging sculpture in a boutique window. A newlywed couple was so struck by the work glistening in the moonlight they paid the selling price of $10,000 without a pause.

A common denominator among these artists is their ability to find alternative measures to promote their art, and be proactive, rather than wait for opportunity to knock. They realized opportunities are everywhere.

Your attitude will get you through the most difficult times. Remind yourself of your many accomplishments and be proud. Don't dwell on your failures or allow yourself to wallow in self-pity. Try a humorous approach, and write a rejection letter, in which you reject the rejection letter you received, and then tear it up. Smile in the face of rejection and look for the lesson. Sometimes, that is of more value than the objective you were trying to achieve.

When one door of happiness closes, another opens;
but often we look so long at the closed door
that we do not see the one which has been opened for us.
Helen Keller

The "o" in No Stands for Opportunity

When you hear the word "no" (and, if you make any strides you will hear it often throughout your career) remember, it is not a death sentence. It is often the beginning in the process of your career growth. Every rejection can be an opportunity to learn from others. You will probably develop many fruitful relationships with people who begin the conversation with "no." Remember, The "o" in "no" stands for opportunity.

These questions hold the power to transform rejections into positive responses:

- In the face of resistance, avoid the temptation to argue, flee, or compromise your integrity. Instead, say with confidence: "I accept your decision. Can you tell me the reason why?"
- Explore possibilities. Try: "I understand you are not interested in the paintings, may I interest you in my works on paper?"
- Obtain specific objections. You might say: "Which aspect of my work are you saying no to – the size, color, or price…?"
- Show empathy and concern for the other person. Say: "I understand that spending $5,000 on an art piece requires more thought. Why don't I call you next week?"
- Try to eliminate obstacles. Say: "Is it the price that concerns you? I would be happy to work out time payments with you."
- The person may not have the authority or ability to make a decision. You might say: "Would you like to discuss it with your spouse or partner and bring him or her with you next time?"
- "No" may mask the fear of making the wrong decision. You might say: "Are you concerned about the size? Do you want me to bring it to your office to see how it will look?"
- Stimulate trust and confidence. Say: "The ABC Corp. bought my work for their lobby. You can see it in their headquarters and get an idea of how the scale would appear in your space."
- Assure the hesitant buyer who needs practical justification for an art purchase. You may say: "My work has increased in value steadily over the past five years. The price for a painting like this will be raised by the gallery in my next exhibition."
- Don't burn your bridges. Secure the green light to keep in touch. Say: "May I send you an invitation to my next Open Studio?"

Chapter 11

Taking Your Art to Market

My favorite clients have always been the ones who collect out of love, just as children collect postage stamps; you fall in love with things that delight you, that you can't resist.
Betty Parsons

You may not understand every nuance of marketing, or have developed any marketing strategies, but you've become aware that there are many roads to choose from in this area, all leading to your ultimate goal – the sale of your work.

The concept of marketing began centuries ago. In the book *Archaic and Classical Greek Art* by Robin Osborne, published by Oxford University Press, there is a chapter titled "Marketing an Image." It refers to the export market in the beginning of the sixth century, when the Greek mainland potters created pottery to compete with markets nearby and, often, far away as North America, the Black Sea, and southern France.

The process of marketing begins as soon as you decide to sell your work. When you advertise your exhibition, and consider the demographics and circulation of the publication, that is one aspect of marketing. When you search for a gallery or an agent, you are taking steps to market your work. When you choose a frame or pedestal for your work, you are considering yet another very important aspect of the marketing process. Whether you are involved in direct sales or have a sales representative or gallery to sell your work, you will benefit from a knowledge of marketing. Artists who fail to attract sales may only need to concentrate more time in marketing their work to make a profound difference.

Most of the artists I've counseled have a desire to receive an income from the sale of their work, but are mystified and unskilled about determining *how, when, where* and *why* to do it and *who* to approach. They will often try to sell their work without a well-planned marketing strategy, and their efforts fall apart. Those artists who ignore marketing will never know why their work is selling, or not.

Marketing your art is merely a different expression of your artistic talents. Once you understand what the full range of these functions are, and how easy they are to incorporate, you can then focus on determining which ones are most effective for you. Marketing is about cause and effect. You should concentrate on achieving the most desired effect.

Marketing, essentially, is not an innate talent. It is developed through acquired skills and practice. Successful marketing involves the collaboration of different elements including a business plan, financial objectives, and presentation materials. It also requires analyzing the attributes of your work and selecting the right audience and avenue for its exposure, publicizing and promoting yourself and the work, and learning sales techniques.

Success in marketing increases with knowledge and resources are readily available. There are many books and workshops for artists which offer simple steps without the hard-sell pressure tactics that are no longer popular. You can also discover good marketing strategies by observing those practiced by successful galleries, museums and artists.

*The practice by which a painter
exhibits his works to the gaze of his fellow citizens
in return for individual remuneration is not new...
If the work is poor, the public taste will soon do it justice.*
Jacques-Louis David (1748-1825)

Identifying Your Market

Determining your special position or *niche* in the market can be achieved by conducting research and using common sense with an awareness of the characteristics of the various art markets. If you have a consistent theme or subject matter and are an expert about your work, which you should be by now, you can be able to ascertain where you and your work will prevail.

A consistent body of work of about twenty or more pieces will help you determine which direction to pursue. If the overall content of your work has many inconsistencies in style, subject matter and content, your efforts will be scattered in more than one direction.

Begin the process with a list of the best and strongest features of your work. Your style, scale, subject matter, medium and price range are all factors that can help to determine in which market areas your work will succeed. Your work may fit into one or more of the following niches: Ethnic, nautical, music, animals, visceral, intellectual, psychological, marine, portraits, historical, healing, visionary, New Age, conservative, traditional, cutting edge, decorative, nature, among others. Make a list of the individuals, businesses, organizations and periodicals that relate directly and indirectly to your work. For example, if your work is nautical your list would include marinas, boat-owners, seafood businesses and restaurants and yachting magazines and their advertisers. Contact them for sales, commissioned work and exhibition opportunities. If you specialize in children's portraits, make a list of all of the children's toy and clothing manufacturers, children's day care centers and orphanages. Offer to exhibit your work, give a demonstration to parents and children, donate a portrait as a raffle at their benefit, offer them a commission to sell the portraits at a fund-raiser event, or arrange cooperative advertising or promotion with them.

Locate market leads by researching telephone and business directories, general and special interest magazines, galleries, museums, organizations, slide registries and companies. Join organizations with common denominators. For example, align yourself with other artists who work in your media, such as the Pastel Society of America, the American Watercolor Society, and the International Sculpture Center. (*See Appendix.2.*)

If you create large, colorful, abstract paintings your work may be more suitable for building lobbies, restaurants and other public spaces in addition to private homes. Your market leads would consist of architects, corporate art consultants and interior designers, among others. If you create small-scale, intimate, animals in terra-cotta, they would be better suited for private collectors, especially those who are animal lovers, and animal-related businesses and organizations.

If your work reflects social or political subject matter, you might investigate alternative, non-profit exhibition spaces and museums to exhibit your work and seek grants in order to expand your concepts in public venues. You can also align yourself with political advocates, special interest groups and activists to bring your message across to the most appropriate audiences.

If you are an animal portrait artist, you have a wide reach of potential buyers and avenues of publicity, including pet owners, breeders, pet groomers, pet food manufacturers, animal shows, pet magazines, greeting card and calendar publishers, and the Franklin Mint, to name a few.

As a painter of florals, your work will comfortably find many sales across the nation in personal collections, offices and public places, as well as provide a possibility for poster production. Other possibilities would be botanical associations, horticulturists, and flower clubs, flower shops, in addition to the local or national chapters of interior designers.

In your approach to finding the best exhibition and sales outlets, consider the following questions: Do you have enough work that reflects a consistent style and/or subject? (Then, you are ready to approach established galleries.) Do you use new technology or new materials? (If so, consider cutting edge galleries and industries.) Does your work deal with healing, spiritual and religious concepts? (Approach "new age" publications, stores, holistic centers and organizations, such as Omega, for leads.) Can your work be organized in series or themes? (If so, consider producing a suite of limited edition prints.) Does your art have historical or cultural significance and therefore have value to a museum, a university, or to a cultural center?

> *Poor artist.*
> *You gave away part of your soul when you painted*
> *the picture which you are now trying to dispose of.*
> Paul Gaughuin

Your Customer Profile

The more you know about the qualities in your work that are most appealing to others, the more accurately you can locate prospective buyers. To develop your customer profile, consider the characteristics of your art that relate to certain individuals, and take a look at your current customers: What kind of people are attracted to your work? Where and how do they live? Are they city or rural inhabitants? Do they fit into a primary educational, ethnic, gender, age, religious or professional group? Where do they buy their art? What periodicals do they read? Where do they spend their vacations? What are their hobbies?

> *Art among a religious group produces reliques;*
> *among a military one, trophies;*
> *among a commercial one, articles of trade.*
> Henry Fuseli

Who and *Where* are the Buyers?

Each year *ARTnews* features their selection of "Top Collectors" and their collections. Many struggling artists believe that this group is the only one they must pursue. That is a defeating prospect since, few of them buy unknown artists' work. When your work is for sale for a few hundred or few thousand dollars, the field is wide open. For your purposes, you should define "collectors" as any individuals or companies that may be interested in your work and are willing to pay the price.

It is important for all of us to dispel many of the mysteries and myths that "collectors" are hiding underground. Buyers of your work are all around you. They are your relatives, friends, friends of relatives and parents of your children's friends. They are the blue collar workers and the people you read about in the social columns. They are people who will come to you and those you must attempt to reach.

Art buyers do not hide under rocks, although you should never leave a stone unturned to find them. You need to develop a network – a coterie of supporters – including artists and friends, not only for camaraderie and encouragement, but also to help you spread the word that your work is available for sale. Make it easy for art buyers to find you. Make yourself visible through artistic endeavors that will attract publicity. Network. Become an expert or spokesperson in your subject matter, style and/or media. Then, the collectors will know where to find you.

> *Today it is the artists*
> *who pull the strings, not the dealers…*
> *the artists are selling themselves at this point.*
> Ileana Sonnabend

Want to meet art buyers? Join museums in the highest categories you can afford and attend their private parties. Sign the guest book mailing list of the best galleries and attend their openings. Join cultural institutions, community service organizations, or the Junior League. Write about the arts in your community newspaper. Open your studio to clubs, charities and tour groups. Make appearances and give talks about your work in colleges, the Chamber of Commerce, hospitals, and other associations. Get a job in a gallery or work for a successful artist. Form or join an organization for artists and recruit well-known collectors, curators and critics to jury your exhibitions.

Continue to expand your market through direct sales, advertising, publicity, networking, volunteer work, fund-raisers, public speaking and teaching. These are all activities that lead to developing name recognition which always affects how the value of your art work is perceived.

Some artists who live outside the cities seek opportunities in the convenience of their own neighborhoods. When Robert's friends were trying to sell their house he hung his art in their living room to be viewed by prospective buyers. He left his business cards and brochures available to those who attended their "Open House." He offered his friend a commission. During the selling process two paintings were sold. The buyer of the house purchased what paintings were left.

Susan scans her neighborhood for "For Sale" signs and approaches the new home owners with a small sketch of their house as a welcome gift. Her friendly gesture has culminated in several painting sales. She has developed relationships with several residential real estate brokers who have commissioned her to execute drawings to use in their sales brochures. Her telephone number is listed on the brochure for inquiries. She also works with commercial brokers who lead her to corporate sales.

Building Your Mailing List

Build your target marketing list steadily and purposefully. Your mailing list begins with relatives, personal friends, professional associates and everyone who has ever bought your work or expressed an interest in your work. They also include every individual who has been a part of your artistic development, including your art instructors, framers and art supply stores.

Methods of increasing your mailing lists are many. Begin with people who have seen your work. Use guest books at your exhibitions and Open Studio events. Have a glass bowl in the exhibition space and invite people to drop in their business card to enter a drawing for a prize.

When you advertise your art work in a magazine or newspaper, offer to send a free brochure or information about you and your work to anyone who shows interest.

Obtain leads of prospective buyers and galleries through general as well as special interest publications. When you determine your customer profile, either subscribe to those same-minded publications or develop leads free by copying them from publications found in your local library.

Circulate brochures and exhibition announcements in your local banks, libraries, hotel concierge desks in luxury hotels, luxury apartment buildings, pedigree pet groomers, tanning salons, airports, beauty salons, travel agencies and universities.

Locate market leads in membership directories, which many organizations offer to non-members for a fee, such as the American Society of Interior Designers. Many special interest magazines also offer sell their subscription lists. Increase prospects by using national and international biographical reference books, such as *Who's Who* Directories. *Crain's New York Business'* annual "Top Business Lists" features names and addresses of the 100 highest paid executives; leading architectural, accounting and law firms; advertising agencies; banks; and fastest-growing firms. Also, visit your local library or use the internet for innumerable resources. ArtNetwork, publishes two comprehensive reference books, *Art Marketing Sourcebook* and *Art Marketing 101*. They also offer numerous mailing lists for artists to purchase. For information call: (530) 470-0862 or visit their website http://artmarketing.com.

Success is what sells.
Andy Warhol

A Marketing Success Story

Maria is a California artist who approached us about advertising her work in *Manhattan Arts International* magazine. She had established herself in her local community and accumulated several one-person and group exhibitions over a ten-year period. Her exceptional paintings paid homage to the laborers of Latin America. They had a universal appeal, and many professionals encouraged her to create limited edition prints. She had a few gallery outlets that she could rely on for sales, but they were not substantial enough to warrant the expense of self-publishing at an initial investment of $3,000 in printing costs.

Maria devised a successful marketing plan. First, she selected the most popular four images that she would consider for creating prints. We featured all four in the magazine with an article that announced that the artist would be printing limited edition prints. Her name and address were listed in the article welcoming inquiries from dealers and buyers. In addition we printed an "overrun" of 1,000 copies of the article in full color. Maria also procured a target market list from the biographical directory *Who's Who in the Latin American Community* to whom she mailed the color sheets with order forms. The combined program led her to several university and museum exhibitions, and hundreds of sales.

Contributing to Maria's success was the *niche* market that she targeted and reached in a very direct and calculated manner. The project required a commitment of finances and time, but there was little risk, and big potential payoff. Even if she had not made a single sale her work received exposure to every Latin American leader as well as to the magazine's international audience.

The Corporate Challenge

A corporation's interest in art is most often to build a collection of work that adheres to the highest standards, while it also must consider the needs and style of its own corporate personality.

Your work may be very suitable for corporate collections if it addresses two or more of the following needs: Does it reflect and enhance the corporate image of the company? Does it decorate the walls and improve the working environment and productivity? Does it fulfill the percent-for-law requirements? Does it qualify as a sound investment? Does it provoke thinking while it's pleasing to the viewers? Does it boost morale?

In addition to providing these assets to the corporation, the purchase of the art must appease the stockholders, who often look askance at buying art as an unnecessary expense, and the art must satisfy the employees who might prefer that the money be spent on salary hikes. Especially now, with corporate downsizing so prevalent, corporations that are cutting out jobs do not want to appear as if they're spending too much money on art.

Corporations use one of two methods for developing their collections. They either have inside personnel that buy art directly from artists and galleries, or they hire outside corporate art consultant firms that specialize in providing art for companies. To locate them, use *ARTnews International Directory of Corporate Art Collections,* available on disc or hard copy. It lists the companies that collect art, what kind of art they collect, status of their collection, and the contact's name. For other leads, follow the annual fall surveys of *Art & Auction* and *Art & Antiques* magazine listing to find out about the specifics relating to America's most active corporate collections. Caroll Michels, author of *How to Survive & Prosper as an Artist* and artist career advisor, publishes *The Newsletter*, available by subscription, in which she lists art consultants. She also offers names and addresses of 600 art consultants on disk. *(See Appendix 4.)*

Don't be timid about contacting corporations directly. Obtain information from the switchboard of the company's policy about collecting art. Find out the name of the art director, art consultant, public relations manager, or corporate communications director. Inquire into the nature of the program and the appropriate way to make one's work known. When you speak to the individual in charge, find out what materials are required and what kind of art they're looking for. Contact that person with a cover letter, photographs and or slides, resume, and a SASE.

Do not limit yourself to targeting established collections. Look for new companies that are being formed in your vicinity with empty walls and contact those companies that you already have sold your work to and who are thinking about expanding in size and relocating. Also, contact architects and interior designers who have corporate clients.

It is always easier to get your work into collections after you have made a few sales. Many artists begin their corporate sales through friends and relatives who place the art work in their offices.

When approaching art consultants and corporate art buyers, you should be prepared with the benefits your art will have on the work environment and how it will enhance the company's image. The same way you would link the special qualities of your work with the similar tastes of individuals and with gallery owners, you will determine the types of businesses that would respond favorably to your work. Interviews with business owners will inform you of their tastes and the type of image they want to project. Articles and advertisements are excellent leads for prospective business buyers. Prospects are to be found in general and special interest publications.

You should consider using Photo CDs as marketing tools to send to corporate art buyers. They are gaining in popularity, as more people are using computers with CD-Roms for both professional and home use. The disks may also be sent to individual art collectors as well as dealers and require less postage than a package of slides and other materials. Artists Space, one of the largest slide registries in the United States, located in New York City, has changed its format from slides to Photo CDs. *(See Appendix.)*

Don't be easily discouraged. At first, you might sell a small, low-priced work to a company, but later, you can introduce them to more valuable works. Remember, it is all a part of an educational process. Marge is a successful artist who began selling limited edition prints of her originals to companies. Before long, the corporate executives and the employees began to show interest in seeing her originals. She is now selling her paintings for several thousand dollars and she no longer depends on the prints for financial support.

When a sale is made to a corporation remember to include it on your resume in a prominent position. You will discover that the "Collections" section will begin to attract more interest in your work.

Feng Shui

Feng Shui is an ancient practice that helps to balance the energy flow in our environment. It has become very popular in our culture within the last few years. Individuals, architects and corporations enlist the services of Feng Shui specialists who design their office and home environments.

It explains why we instinctively feel more comfortable in some locations opposed to others; how the places in which we live and work affect the way we feel; and how even minor adjustments in our environment – the placement of our easel or desk, or the choices of color and materials in specific areas – can have a positive impact on our effectiveness and attitude.

There are several books written on Feng Shui including *Feng Shui at Home* by Carol Soucek King. (*See Appendix.*) The subject is worth investigating, especially if you want to improve your living and working environments and bring more harmony and comfort into your life. It will also reveal how the colors, forms and shapes of the art you create may have impact on others. This knowledge can serve as a useful marketing tool.

In 1980, when AIPAD hosted its first annual trade show in New York City with 40 exhibitors, there were approximately 200 guests. Attendance for the 1998 show was well over 7,000 visitors.
Donna Cameron

Finding Markets through Art Fairs

Art fairs and expositions take place world-wide. Some expositions present the work of art dealers only, others offer individual artists the opportunity to set up their own booths and sell their work directly to the art trade and to the public. Some of these shows cater to the decorative and commercial artworks; others have higher quality standards and focus on original works of art and more valuable limited edition prints.

Attending expositions can offer you an education and lead to marketing contacts. Artists who are interested in locating print publishers and out-of-town galleries will find an art fair to be a productive visit. You will also learn how other artists promote themselves in their booth displays and printed materials, and how they frame and price their work. Observe how fine art businesses market, present, price and promote. Pick up samples of catalogs and postcards and, pick up leads. Distribute your own.

Many fairs hold symposiums during the show, featuring panel discussions in which experts in the fields talk about a range of subjects from current market trends in art to collecting and selling. These events also offer networking opportunities.

New York's "Art Expo" is a show that takes place at the Jacob Javits Convention Center every March. Increasingly, artists have been setting up their own booths in this venue. Some artists are able to support themselves throughout the year from the commissions and contacts they make at one show. However, it is an expensive proposition. An exhibition booth of ten square feet can cost thousands of dollars. At first, you may want to arrange to show some of your work with other artists, or better yet, with a gallery. Attend the show before committing yourself and observe which artists are more successful and why. Interview artists to find out how beneficial it may be for you.

In addition to "Art Expo" in New York, there is "Art Chicago" in May at the Navy Pier – a much higher scale exposition featuring over 200 of the world's leading galleries from 25 countries, attracting 40,000 visitors. There is also the popular "The Outsider Art Fair" which features galleries of outsider, naive, self-taught, art brut, visionary, and intuitive art, in the Puck Building, in January, in New York City. "The National Black Fine Art Show" at the Puck Building in January is also worth a visit. "The Photography Show", the world's largest art fair devoted to fine art photography, is presented by the Association of International Photography Art Dealers at the Hilton Hotel in February. A high caliber international art fair is "The Art Show", that takes place at The Seventh Regiment Armory on Park Avenue in February. It presents the members of the Art Dealers Association of America (ADAA), a prestigious membership organization of the nation's leading dealers.

For additional information on art fairs check your national art publications for listings and locate resource books such as a book titled *The Art Fair Source Book. (See Appendix.)*

My art tries to make observations for which
commissioned work generally gives no room and
in which fantasy and invention have no limit.
Francisco de Goya

Markets for Your Work are Everywhere
80 Venues and Resources from A to Z

1. Accountants
2. Airports
3. Animal rights groups
4. Architects
5. Art consultants
6. Art organizations
7. Art publishers
8. Banks
9. Book publishers
10. Botanical clubs
11. Boutiques
12. Bus terminals
13. Chambers of Commerce
14. Charities
15. Churches
16. Commissioned works
17. Consulates and Embassies
18. Corporations
19. Country Clubs
20. Cruise ships
21. Community centers
22. Dance halls
23. Day care centers
24. Dog Breeders
25. Diners
26. Doctor's offices
27. Educational organizations
28. Entertainment clubs
29. Fairs/Festivals
30. Franklin Mint
31. Federal Halls
32. Fire stations
33. Fitness Clubs
34. Flower shops
35. Framers
36. Furniture showrooms
37. Galleries
38. Gift shops
39. Gov't agencies
40. Greeting Card Publishers
41. Guilds
42. Hair Salons
43. Hotels
44. Hospitals
45. Holistic Centers
46. Health spas
47. Insurance agents
48. Interior Designers
49. Internet
50. Juried Competitions
51. Law offices
52. Libraries
53. Mail order catalogues
54. Marinas
55. Medical facilities
56. Model homes
57. Motels
58. Museums
59. Night clubs
60. Open Studios
61. Periodicals
62. Pet Shops
63. Print Publishers
64. Real estate brokers
65. Resorts
66. Restaurants
67. Senior Citizen Centers
68. Slide Registries
69. Spas
70. Specialty markets
71. Store windows
72. Subway stations
73. Swim clubs
74. Synagogues
75. Tanning salons
76. Therapists
77. Travel agencies
78. Universities
79. *Who's Who* Directories
80. Wineries

Chapter 12

Successful Selling

*There is too much talk and gossip;
pictures are apparently made, like stock-market prices,
by competition of people eager for profits...
All this traffic sharpens our intelligence
and falsifies our judgment.*
Edgar Degas

The thought of selling makes your stomach turn and can cause your heart to palpitate. You envision loud, street corner hawkers, obnoxious, fast-talking car salesmen, pushy women at the cosmetic counter – all making false promises. This is the last type of person you want to become.

During those blissful years in art school, no one ever warned you that one day you would be faced with this dilemma. You'd rather spend the time negotiating the aesthetics of color, design, form and texture rather than discuss the benefits of your work to a prospective buyer.

The first step to financial security is the acceptance that your perception of selling may be a big deterrence. Financial success begins with awareness of prosperity and a positive focus of selling. Selling is an enjoyable process of exchange, not unlike, when you traded baseball cards or marbles as a kid.

When you sell your work to others, you are offering them the opportunity to own something that will enrich their lives. The selling of art begins with an awareness and expression of its benefits. Rejoice in the fact that art has communicative and healing powers. It has the power to educate and can significantly alter viewer's attitudes and behaviors. When someone buys your work, a permanent bond is formed. You should thoroughly savor the joyful process of sharing and exchanging it for money and recognition.

Money earned from work that has been sold may offer you financial freedom from the job you loathe, or an unhappy marriage, either of these may currently be your sole or major support. The sale of a work of art also proves that you and your art have the power to captivate an individual. The sale of art work perpetuates the circle of communication – the reason why so many artists become artists in the first place.

Want to Increase Sales?
You May Need to Reject Some Myths

Myth #1: "In order to sell my work I have to be aggressive."

Hard-selling, aggressive tactics are no longer acceptable or effective. The best salespeople are assertive – not aggressive. (There is a major difference.) They exude confidence, elicit trust, express themselves in a personable and enthusiastic manner, and are truly interested in the prospective buyers' thoughts and desires. Professionals place their customer's best interests ahead of their own; they don't use force or coercion to close the sale.

If you want to sell your artwork, the best resources you can use are sincerity, knowledge, politeness, resourcefulness, empathy, confidence and enthusiasm.

> *I would sooner look for figs on thistles*
> *than for the higher attributes of art from one*
> *whose ruling motive in its pursuit is money.*
> Asher B. Durand

Myth #2: "I wasn't born a salesperson."

Selling is not always an innate talent. It involves skills that can be learned, developed and sharpened. Desire and motivation are key factors to attaining selling skills. Your energy will drive and sustain your commitment. Become a devoted student in this area. Take the time to understand the reasons why people buy art. The more you know about the prospective buyer, the stronger your position – such as their lifestyle, where they come from, likes and dislikes, art they already own, favorite artists and hobbies. Continue to improve your skills by reading books and taking courses on the art of non-aggressive selling.

Excellent sales teachers are all around you. Observe the skills of successful art dealers and artists, and those you respect and trust, then adopt those behaviors that make you feel most comfortable. The best skills are those that enhance your personality and feel natural to you. Practice will lead to fruition.

Myth #3: "The art should sell by itself."

So many artists wish that this was true and how sadly misinformed they are. Many art buyers may not relate to your work in the same manner in which it was created. The reasons why people buy art run the gamut – from matching the carpet to acquiring social status. Not everyone understands art or has confidence in their own judgment, which is why they seek the counsel of art advisors, dealers and other collectors. As an artist, you can encourage them to trust their responses and back them up by emphasizing your achievements. Reassure them that you understand their hesitancy, and that the art they own is an extension of themselves, therefore valid and appropriate.

According to an article in *Entrepreneur* magazine on the subject of marketing, understanding the laws of psychology is helpful if you want to increase your sales. Theoretically people are either left-brained or right-brained. Left-brained people are receptive to sequential, logical information and respond to the kind of sales techniques that gives them ten reasons to buy. (Such as: "One of the ten reasons why you should buy this painting is it will increase in value...") Right-brained people are more receptive to emotional and aesthetic appeals ("The undulating waves in this painting are sensual and evoke a sense of peace and harmony..."). You may want to incorporate elements in your written marketing materials and verbal conversation during sales presentations that will attract both left- and right-brained people!

For art to be sold, it must be talked about with enthusiasm, it must be praised, and its value must be explained. A strong resume, reviews and attractive visual and editorial documentation are your sales tools. You should create brochures, fliers, color postcards and/or folded cards and have them with you at all times. An effective marketing piece is an 8-1/2" x 11" color sheet with one or more images displayed on it with your name, address, and telephone, a brief and positive description of your work, and a brief biography. You may also add a favorable quote from a critic. Develop the best quality promotional materials that you can afford and distribute them with pride.

There are several printers that specialize in artists' sales materials and the following companies are recommended by artists. Call and ask for sample kits and price lists and compare the quality and prices with your local printers. Art Editions (800) 331-8449. Post Script Press (800) 511-2009. Color Card (800) 875-1386. Modern Postcard (800) 959-8365. Color Q (800) 999-1007. Mitchell Graphics (800) 841-6793.

Any fool can paint a picture,
but it takes a wise man
to be able to sell it.
Samuel Butler

Myth #4: "To sell my work I have to boast and brag."

Modest self-promotion in the form of pointing out your career accomplishments, such as awards, exhibitions, and other collectors that own your work, is a process of sharing information. It helps the customer to feel confident about making a decision to buy your work. If talking about your career credentials embarrasses you, the process will be much easier if you have sales and promotional materials to present to them. If properly prepared, these materials will do the talking for you. If you don't have any materials, you should make an effort to create them. You will find it difficult to sell your work without them. How many substantial purchases have you made without reading any literature describing the assets of the product?

Myth #5: "Selling involves taking money from someone."

Contrary to the misconception many people have that selling is *taking* something *from* people, it is actually an activity of *sharing with* people. A successful sales presentation begins with a friendly greeting, then a rapport and proceeds to establish confidence in the art and the seller through a positive presentation and an exchange of ideas through mutual respect and integrity, and ends with a final close.

The best sale is when the buyer feels they have received more than they have given. You see, when you sell your work you are actually placing it with someone who will now appreciate its value and whose life will be enriched by it. As your sales grow, so will your confidence and reassurance – assets that will propel you to future buyers.

Myth #6: "Only rich, educated people buy art. I don't know any collectors."

As an artist I must have sold hundreds of pieces of art work directly to the buyers, and most of them I can't remember. Twenty years later, however, I can vividly recall two of my most memorable sales. One was an 80 year-old woman, living on a fixed-income, and the other was a 16 year-old student who came from a low-income family. For both of them my paintings represented their first art purchases.

I will never forget the look of bliss on the face of the elderly woman when she stood in front of my landscape painting and released herself to it. It reminded her of a place she knew as a child and brought her solace. She felt a strong connection with it and was compelled to buy it. I will always cherish the special feelings we shared when we made the exchange. As for the other sale to the student, I was surprised and elated when she told me she took a part-time job to pay for her painting. She paid me in weekly installments and always in person, so she could visit her painting. When she completed her payments, she invited me to her home to see the special place where she hung the work.

By participating in the direct selling process on these occasions, I was richly rewarded – beyond any financial goals. If I hadn't made the paintings accessible to them and engaged them in dialogue, I am sure these purchases would not have occurred, and I would have missed the opportunity of sharing special moments.

I also learned never to judge people at first glance. Everyone – wealthy or not – is a potential customer.

There are no dumb customers.
Peter Drucker

Do a little more each day than you think you possibly can.
Lowell Thomas

Selling Your Art in an Exhibition

Have you ever wondered why the most successful artists' gallery exhibitions are nearly or completely sold out before the show even opens? Did you think it was luck? Think again. Hard work brought about those sales long before opening night.

Many artists come to me for a consultation at the end of their exhibitions to express the agony of having nothing to show except a pile of bills. My question is, what efforts did they make to avoid their anguish? Many artists rarely give a thought to selling until their exhibition opens, however, the art of selling should be an integral part of their careers twelve months a year.

Unless you are fortunate to be represented by a highly established and aggressive gallery with a strong marketing plan, I suggest that you implement some sales and marketing plans months ahead of your exhibition. The marketing activities begin the day the date is set in writing. The planning stages begin by marking all essential activities and deadlines on your calendar. The moment the date is set in writing, start spreading the word!

In a non-commercial gallery venue, in which you are in charge of your own sales, start selling the work before the exhibition opens by showing prospective collectors photographs of your work, inviting them to the studio, and discussing your exhibition. Some artists offer special pre-exhibition "Open Studio" events to build anticipation and cultivate pre-exhibition sales among their existing collectors. Many art buyers are delighted to see the work of art they own on display with the red dot indicating "sold" next to it. This red mark of success also helps to encourage further sales.

For your opening reception, hire or recruit an experienced sales person who will assist you with the sales and paper work, while you can relax and concentrate on meeting as many agents, dealers, writers and prospective buyers as possible. Be cordial to everyone who attends the event, but don't waste time talking to many unqualified buyers. When speaking to prospective buyers keep the conversation focused on the artwork that interests them.

You and your assistant should collect the names, addresses and phone numbers of qualified leads. After the opening reception follow up on serious prospects and continue to follow up on prospects during and after the exhibition.

During the weeks or months of your exhibition plan many group activities in the gallery. Invite special interest groups to hold their meetings and receptions in the exhibition space to increase your show's visibility. Organize events that will attract the educated and affluent, as well as the press. Arrange "Meet The Artist" events and list them as "free and open to the public" in the local newspapers, radio and TV stations. Invite student classes, charity organizations and other special interest groups to meet you while you discuss your work, and perhaps do a demonstration.

If to increase sales is one of your priorities, it is better to do fewer shows more efficiently than many shows with no strategies. It is far better to have one less work finished or framed by the time the show opens than to neglect crucial time cultivating the attendance and motivating interest in your show.

If art is to survive as an important language,
it will be through the persistent will of artists
and through models chosen from among themselves.
Harold Rosenberg

Everyone lives by selling something.
Robert Lewis Stevenson

Successful Selling Techniques

The Artist's Newsletter

People like to own successful artists' work. By sharing your accomplishments you are getting your collectors more involved and encouraging more sales. Many artists know this which is why the artist's newsletter is growing in popularity. A previous task now made easy by computers, these newsletters keep us abreast of the artist's activities, commissions, up-coming shows, awards and new works in progress.

Carole Davis sent me a simple easy-to-read "Update", which lists her achievements month-to-month. Anthony Whelihan mails "The Word on Whelihan", an ambitious quarterly newsletter, complete with photographs of his collectors and columnists at his opening receptions. Gaye Elise Beda mails a friendly and enthusiastic "End of the Year Wrap-Up" promotion to everyone on her mailing list. This practice has led to sales, exhibitions and general increased interest in her work. Well-known sculptor Carole A. Feuerman recently mailed to me her "Feuerman Studios", a fact-filled newsletter that promotes her activities and sells her sculpture and new book, in a soft-sell, exuberant style, complete with an order form.

Your newsletter doesn't have to be a form of top journalism. Let the pictures do the talking, and get the word out. If you can't write well, recruit a friend to edit.

More Selling Strategies

- To increase sales, Bill inserts his announcement cards for his exhibitions in envelopes when he pays his bills. This method has brought him more than a few sales and other kinds of opportunities, such as an offer to present a slide lecture.

- Industry-related businesses make excellent clients. Susan reported that she sold several of her paintings of European scenes to a travel agency for their corporate offices. Their satellite offices sell her framed, limited edition prints right from the walls and give them as gifts to their best customers. Keeping in mind the importance of targeting her market, she advertises her art in travel and hotel magazines.

- In November a cooperative gallery presents a "Small Works Holiday Show" with every work of art priced below $250. Each year they select a children's charity to which they contribute a portion of the proceeds. Many of the sales transpire because of the goodwill behind the event. The buyer gains a beautiful work of art and a portion of the sale price is tax deductible.

- Doug created a series of mixed media abstract works that were inspired by computerized images. Although they were abstract images, he assigned titles to them that industry professionals would relate to, such as "Bytes", "External Bay", and "Interface." He approached every computer-related company in his area and landed several exhibitions and sales. He also selected one of his most popular designs and had it printed on mouse pads with his name, email and website. One company bought an original work and ordered several dozen corresponding mouse pads which it distributed to its employees as gifts.

- Elizabeth and five of her artist friends design an annual calendar. Each of them has two of their art works featured in two months of the calendar. They share the printing costs and divide the printed calendars to sell and/or give away.

- To announce his exhibition, Eduardo sent out reproductions of one of his black and white drawings with an invitation encouraging his guests to color it and bring it to the opening reception. It raised his guests' curiosity to see his drawing hanging in the show and to compare it with theirs.

There's no such thing as "hard sell" and "soft sell."
There is only "smart sell" and "stupid sell."
Leo Burnett

- Hold an "Open Studio" and invite people to enjoy a behind-the-scenes tour of your work space. Create a casual, clean, safe and uncluttered environment in which they can browse through your work. Supply plenty of promotional materials and price lists.
- Rent your work. Many artists are discovering this is a way to augment their income, and it is an ideal arrangement for the buyer and the seller, especially in sluggish economic times. Prepare a written contract. Offer the renter the option to buy at any time. Consider joining other artists and establish an art rental association. Prospects should include individuals as well as law firms, medical spaces, restaurants and real estate offices. Make sure that the first installment is substantial enough to cover insurance if the renter does not carry insurance.
- Barter your work for professional services, such as legal, accounting, medical, advertising and printing.

James has been bartering his work with a local restaurant. The arrangement is very convenient when he entertains a collector from out of town. One painting paid for ten dinners.

Steven has avoided paying his tax advisor for seven years. In late March, while the rest of us are having panic attacks, he delivers his documents and receipts to have his documents prepared. His advisor receives a beautiful new painting in exchange for his efforts.

For barter companies, look in the Yellow Pages under Barter and Trade Exchange.

If you engage in barter, remember to follow the appropriate tax rules.

After The Sale

Marketing experts concur that it takes five times the effort to acquire new clients than to repeat a sale to an existing client. They also state twenty percent of your collectors will produce eighty percent of your sales. Individual contacts and links to key groups that are already familiar with you are infinitely more beneficial than large direct mail campaigns to those people who don't know you. In your efforts to seek greener pastures, you may be neglecting the best resources in your back yard. Whenever you make a sale, it should mark the beginning of a long, rewarding relationship, if you pay attention.

How do you keep the loyalty of your collectors? Start by giving the buyers a bonus, such as a list of tips for caring for the work. This might include special matting, framing and hanging instructions, or transporting methods. They will appreciate the gesture and will remember your expertise and thoroughness.

A month after a sale, ask them how they are enjoying the new acquisition. They may share wonderful feedback and may respond by recommending future purchases and/or clients.

Make an effort to continuously increase the customer's perception of the value of your work. Make them feel important. Share your new projects with them, send them visuals, and remind them of your accomplishments: They will probably tell their friends about the wise investment they made, which will bring new prospective customers to you. Continue to keep them informed about all of your achievements before, during and in-between exhibitions. Reach out to them through holiday cards with images of your work reproduced on them.

Think of ways to encourage increased sales. Wouldn't the owners of your paintings and sculpture love to own a small drawing, monoprint, limited edition print or sculpture, silk-screened T-shirt or note cards, created by you? Let them know that you are always creating something new for them to enjoy!

Before you release your work, you may want to ask the buyer to allow you to borrow the work back for brief periods for important exhibitions. Also agree to get resale information, should they decide to transfer the work to another owner. Agree to a royalty on re-transfer of artwork. Get all of this in writing.

> *Many early collectors stopped buying*
> *when prices skyrocketed into another orbit,*
> *leaving the market open for younger collectors.*
> Leo Castelli

Understanding the Resistance to Buying Art

The factors that influence the art market have changed over the decades. During the 60s and 70s, many people bought art to hedge against inflation. "The 80s Boom" was characterized by high prices and over-valued art. It led to what may be called "The 90s Bust", causing over-zealous dealers and artists to send many art buyers running away, clutching onto their wallets in fear of being sold the next flavor of the month.

Those in search of art want trustworthy, intelligent, service-oriented people to advise them. As a result, the artist today, who takes an interest and invests some time to educate, share and win over the trust and confidence of the art buyers, will be richly rewarded.

The prospective buyer of your art needs information and looks to you for guidance. Ask questions and listen to their responses. If the buyer is hesitant your questions will lead to the reasons why the individual is holding back. The experience should be comfortable, not confrontational. If you are helpful and supportive, and not defensive and egotistical, the buyer will accept your credibility and your chances for the sale will be positive. As with any other purchase they must be convinced that your work is worthy of the price you are asking. If you show integrity and back up the value of your work with evidence they will be more likely to be assured of its merit.

> *The best way to have a good idea*
> *is to have a lot of ideas.*
> Linus Pauling

Many wise artists practice the art of diversification. You increase your sale's volume by offering different price levels, and thereby reach a broader segment of the population. For instance, in addition to selling original art at hundreds and thousands of dollars, introduce other options in the $100-500 range, such as limited edition prints, drawings and monoprints. Sell works on paper along with larger canvases. Sell photographs and videos of your installations. Sell small sculpture or wearable art in addition to your larger bronzes.

Technology has rapidly advanced the quality of limited edition prints with the introduction of digital prints and Fine Art Iris Prints, also called Giclées. They are high-resolution prints that can be reproduced with superb accuracy on acid-free watercolor paper, stretched canvas or other surfaces. Coatings may be applied to increase water resistance. Artists may add paint or other media to the prints. One of the biggest advantages of digital prints is that artists may order a single print at an affordable price. They may sell signed and numbered, limited edition reproductions of their popular paintings without having to stock pile hundreds of prints.

Naturally, the longevity of digital prints is limited and artists must inform buyers of their impermanence. Prices and quality vary, so I recommend that you research this new area thoroughly. For more information see *Digital Fine Art* magazine and *Art Trends: The Magazine of Fine Art Prints. (See Appendix 4.)*

Pricing Your Work

Artists who are beginning their artistic growth, with a limited sales history, may prematurely venture into the art market. They approach galleries and art buyers expecting open arms and find rejection, instead. Although their relatives and friends might be staunch admirers they may not be qualified to help the artists determine if their work is ready for a larger audience.

It is advisable to obtain some professional guidance from an artist advisor, or other art professional, before you take the leap seriously, regarding the appropriate venue in which to sell, the price to place on your work and other essential tips. That individual can also offer advice regarding the proper way to price your work and its position in the art market.

When determining your prices, be realistic. Do you want to constantly sell work that will steadily increase in value? Has your work passed the test of selling to several art buyers outside your small coterie of friends and relatives? Do you wish to price your work high and be satisfied with a few, infrequent sales, or would you rather price your work modestly and try to appeal to a larger audience? When your art is priced fairly buyers will come back satisfied and willing to pay more as the value of your work increases. It is easier to raise prices than lower them.

In the process of establishing your prices, engage in some market research. Visit galleries and art fairs. Do a comparative study between your work and others in the same style and media as well as the geographic areas in which you will be selling your work. If you are a young artist in Ohio, you can't compare your prices with New York galleries.

Your study should include comparative size, subject matter, technical ability and professional accomplishments. Collect resumes, brochures and price lists of other artists.

Seek out artists who are actually selling their work. Remember, it's the actual selling price that matters, not the asking price. Sometimes original works are set at a high price because artists want to increase the value of the work on the secondary market or increase the sales of the limited editions. Also, keep in mind, high prices for emerging artists are often set by artists who pay for their exhibitions.

What steps can you take to raise the value of your work? Your resume is an excellent place to begin to evaluate how others perceive you. It is essential to know what is important to the art buyers you are trying to reach: Would they pay more for your work if you had a one-person exhibitions in New York or would winning a prestigious national award peak their interest? What holes on your resume need to be filled? What weak spots need to be eliminated? How can you strengthen your position and credibility? Ask other art professionals for suggestions.

Don't wait too long to establish a value for your work. Otherwise, you might find yourself with a large inventory of work and no buyers on your mailing list when you get the opportunity to have an exhibition.

When you start, your price range will be in the low hundreds and low thousands, for which there will be little resistance. If you are involved in direct sales and are selling comfortably at that price, you have to consider whether you are ready for a gallery which will be able to offer you the same price for your work, and take a fifty percent commission.

If your work can only command the price you are currently asking, and no higher in the gallery, it may not be in your best interest to sell through a gallery, in which case you would be receiving only half of the current price. Until your prices reach a steady market value, most of the better galleries would not risk taking your work, because they need to consider their profit margin. As you can see, strategic timing is important.

Chapter 13

The P's & Q's of Public Relations

*Some are born great,
others achieve greatness,
and some hire public relations officers.*
Daniel J. Boorstein

Public Relations is a broad umbrella under which community relations, networking, publicity, promotion and a multitude of other activities fall. We know that Jackson Pollock and Jacob Epstein shared the same public relations agent, Eleanor Lambert, who started a public relations company in 1935, specializing in promoting the careers of artists. The use of public relations, however, is not a new concept; it goes back to Futurism, born in the years immediately preceding World War I. This art movement aimed to agitate an uneasy self-consciousness, and it incorporated advanced techniques of publicity and showmanship.

Public relations work requires time and effort, but it is worth the energy, for it costs less than advertising, and it is perceived with more credibility than advertising. Artists who want to advance their public recognition must consider public relations as an integral part of their successful career plans.

The subject of public relations is discussed in detail in this section with several different strategies. In other parts of the book, especially devoted to relationships and networking, are extremely helpful adjuncts to this chapter. You will also find advice, step-by-step instructions and samples of promotional documents in *Presentation Power Tools For Fine Artists*. The publicity campaign, the publicity process, the best way to create press releases (with several samples), and advice from P.R. professionals are included. *(See order form in the back of the book.)*

> *There's only one thing in the world worse than being talked about, and that is not being talked about.*
> Oscar Wilde

Raise the Volume

You should use creative tools and techniques to raise the volume on self-promotion, and thereby increase the perceived value of their work. Study and select the methods that fit your personality, budget, geographic location and type of art work.

In his desire to attain fame and fortune Jeff Koons has spared no expense; he bought ad space in art magazines and billboard space around New York City. Lynda Benglis bought a two-page spread to spread her nude body in *Artforum*, and painter Marilyn Minter bought TV time to announce her exhibit. They did it unabashedly and triumphantly. Keith Haring took his art to the subways and made his mark on the walls underground, attracting the attention of thousands of commuters and the evening news. Peter Max is an artist who keeps ticking – as the official artist for five Grammy Awards, four Super Bowls, the U.S. Tournament and many other international events. The late Andy Warhol created his own public persona through his many artistic and social activities, and was immediately recognizable with the help of a pale face and a white wig.

> *To see one's name in print!*
> *Some people commit a crime for no other reason.*
> Gustave Flaubert

One way to develop recognition is through controversy. A New York artist who wanted to spread the image of his new cartoon character and escape the high price of advertising, posted 1,000 subway signs throughout New York City without paying a penny. Gannet Transit, the private company that has the contract to sell subway advertising space, immediately sent a crew to rip down the unauthorized posters. Until then, however, the posters had already aroused enormous curiosity. The artist also did a massive mailing of post cards and buttons to the press and smeared stickers on phone booths all over the City. He caught the attention of a *New York Newsday* writer who devoted at least 1,000 words of copy to the artist's delight. Surprisingly, he was never arrested, but I suspect that he would have been pleased if he had if it generated more publicity.

Most artists prefer to take the less controversial route and concentrate on letting their art speak for them, as they steadily strengthen their position in the art world through honors and awards. Others become an impressive voice as arts advocates. Artists who crave the spotlight and want instant success may have a talent to attract attention and become popular figures in the art world. They may choose to attract attention by wearing outrageous clothes or dyeing their hair purple and green. Other artists may simply enjoy having a small group of friends recognize their artistic efforts. Many artists seek international recognition by posting their work on numerous websites.

Different Ways to Shine

Many artists cooperate with other organizations to achieve name recognition by offering a percentage of their exhibition sales to a favorite charity. The organization promotes the exhibition through its contacts. This kind of non-commercial partnership usually attracts the attention of the press.

Christian successfully employed a method of "cross-promotion" when he offered each buyer of his work a gift certificate to be redeemed in a top restaurant. As part of this agreement, the restaurant hung his work and featured the artist's work on the cover of their menu.

The Richmond Galleries in Marblehead, OH organized a "Breakfast with the Artists" series. They offered a free continental breakfast and gifts and invited guests to meet a different guest artist each month at the gallery.

The galleries in the Meat Market District in New York City join forces and promote Meat Market Crawls on Thursday nights, when all of the galleries agree to stay open late.

Lucia approached galleries near her show and suggested placing a cooperative advertisement in the local newspaper. The ad increased her visibility and she saved money.

Dennis has his work silk screened on T-shirts, canvas bags, and note cards, and mounted on magnets, which he sells and gives away as a profitable means of self-promotion.

Mary presents talks and slide presentations to many different special interest groups as a way to promote her work.

*In the future everyone will be famous
for fifteen minutes.*
Andy Warhol

Getting Your Fifteen Minutes

Publicity is media exposure – in the form of print, radio, TV or the internet, and offers many benefits. Publicity makes more people aware of you and your art work, which leads to sales and other career opportunities. It is a vehicle to gain the attention of galleries, collectors, grant-givers and critics. As your reputation grows, so does the commitment from those individuals who already support you and your work.

There are many opportunities to receive publicity. Main categories that you will want to consider on your media list are daily and weekly newspapers, local news bureaus, bureau offices of national media, monthly newspapers, art publications, wire services, websites, specialty publications, foreign language publications and periodicals, social press, freelance writers and radio and television stations. *Bacon's Newspaper/Magazine Directory, Editor and Publisher International Yearbook* and *Literary Market Place* are comprehensive resources that list magazines, newspapers, and radio and TV stations and proper contact names and addresses. They can be found in your library.

In the beginning, your media list will just be a collection of names, but once you follow up with telephone calls and familiarize yourself with the writers and their needs, you will find yourself establishing a rewarding relationship with them.

Help the reporters do their job. Mail press releases that they can use in their entirety. Send attractive visual materials. Return their calls promptly. Have background information on you and your art work available for quick faxing. Be cordial and professional.

Keep your media list updated frequently. Make phone calls periodically to confirm if the individuals are still affiliated with the media, or if there have been changes in positions.

> *Manet did not do the expected.*
> *He was a pioneer. He followed his individual whim.*
> *Told the public what he wanted it to know, not the time worn things the public already knew and thought it wanted to hear again.*
> *The public was very much offended.*
> Robert Henri

The promotional materials that create your press kit reflect your degree of professionalism and commitment to your work. Pay attention to every detail, including the quality of the letterhead, the type style and size, the clarity of your message and the neatness of the overall package. If any part of it appears unkempt, the recipient may lose interest. Don't forget to send visuals; pictures tell more than words, and they will increase your chances of getting media placement.

Know the deadlines and send materials in time to meet them. Send a thank you letter to writers who include you in a review or article, no matter how much "ink" you received.

Many trade publications welcome contributors with knowledge. Suggest a story idea on a subject related to art and offer an outline or a few paragraphs. If you live in a small community, offer to be the art reporter for the local paper or radio show. If you live in a large city, cover the section of the city about which you are most familiar. Also, write "Letters to the Editor" of all publications when you feel the impulse to do so! Make sure that your name and all other pertinent biographical information is added. If they run your article, you may be considered an expert and receive a surge of credibility.

Read the special columns in your regional and national periodicals and look for angles. To attract publicity, create a story that is about your career. Did you recently retire as a dentist to become a full-time artist? Did you win an important award or grant? Did you finish an intriguing commission? Is your work controversial? Have you been featured in all local papers, radio programs and local TV? Have you had a one-person show in the best university? Did you receive an award from your mayor for your outstanding artistic contributions to the community?

To increase your income and establish recognition, offer a seminar, demonstration, class or workshop. Local news media will often cover an interesting topic, and it's a great way to generate publicity. Charge little or no admission, have great handouts and bring slides of your work to project during your talk and bring some of your art work. High schools, colleges, art groups, museums, galleries, civic groups, Chambers of Commerce, Rotary Clubs, church groups, political groups and other institutions invite artists to lecture individually or to serve on panel discussions. In many instances, your work may be on exhibition during the presentation. Make an effort to have the occasion photographed or videotaped for future use. The artist who offers a lecture with the exhibition is often viewed as an asset to museums and galleries.

Time your publicity or exhibition to concur with major events or organizations that are related to your work. Coordinating your efforts with highly recognized groups can offer huge benefits. As Editor-in-Chief of *Manhattan Arts International* magazine I have hosted many events to promote the Arts, such as "Salute to French Art and Culture", Salute to Greek Art and Culture" and "Salute to Italian Art and Culture", in which I joined forces with the respective consulates and art groups. One year during American Music Week I organized a "Salute to American Music Week" gala in a large New York night club. I invited music personalities from classical to jazz to rock, including Beverly Sills, Wynton Marsalis and Frank Zappa to accept *Manhattan Arts* American Music Awards. The event attracted thousands of attendees and received national television, radio and print coverage. On another occasion I organized the first *Manhattan Arts* political debate among Manhattan's candidates for Borough President and asked Tony Randall to moderate. Leaders from all disciplines of the Arts and the press were in attendance. The event brought attention to the important issues facing the Arts and overnight it placed the magazine in front of a large influential audience. Another memorable event was when we presented an exhibition of Ken Duncan's photographs in a major New York gallery to raise money for the Performing Arts Center for Health.

To heighten your publicity time your art exhibitions to coincide with national events that relate strongly to your work's content and subject matter. For example, October: Breast Cancer Awareness; February: Black History Month; March: Women's History Month; and don't forget that Earth Day is April 22.

Ask for your favorite publications' "Editorial Calendars" for opportunities to submit subject-related materials for free publicity. For example, the March-April issue of *Manhattan Arts International* celebrates Women in the Arts, with a special reception in coordination with the issue. The May-June issue focuses on "The Artful Traveler." We ask artists to submit brief descriptions of how travel has inspired their work, accompanied by photographs of those works. The July-August issue is devoted to our Annual Competition. We have another issue that features artists whose work is involved with healing. Artists who keep abreast of our annual activities prepare for such events.

Exhaust every possible avenue of publicity and form of recognition you can tap in your region. When you obtain some success in a major city, you can bring it back to boost your career in your home town. An artist, who received publicity in a national art magazine, sent the article with press releases to every media outlet and was featured on the cover of the local town paper and had interviews on radio and television. Another artist living in the state of Washington, who was featured in *Manhattan Arts* magazine, organized a "magazine signing" and exhibition at a local Barnes & Noble bookstore.

> *No act of kindness,*
> *no matter how small, is ever wasted.*
> Aesop

Volunteer for P.R. Success

Look for opportunities to be generous. Think of all of those individuals who are less fortunate than you. You don't have to look far to notice that many people are suffering from fatalities and diseases. By giving of yourself, your talent and your time, you will be pleasantly surprised. You will not only feel fulfilled because you are helping others, you will also be creating a positive public image. And the more you give of yourself, the more you will have to give!

Don't wait for a charity to approach you. Contact them with an idea which includes the donation of your work, your time and, possibly, your services. Share your creativity and talent in ways that are useful to the organizations' efforts to raise funds. Art is a vehicle with which they can communicate their statement of purpose.

Follow your heart and passions, and they will lead you to special interest groups that share your concerns. Whatever your preference, there are groups to join – computer technology, politics, anti-censorship, health care, seniors, Pro-life vs Pro-choice, anti-drugs, gun control, to name a few. Volunteer to help in hospitals, libraries, museums, the city council, political clubs, neighborhood improvement groups, PTA, girl scouts, religious and cultural groups, the Better Business Bureau, Chamber of Commerce, Kiwanis, variety club, United Way, animal protection groups, small business clubs, breakfast clubs, business associations and your neighborhood business groups.

When you approach a charity organization to offer your services, be patient and consistent and get involved on a regular basis. At first, you may have to begin at an entry level before the charity's board of directors listens to your ideas. If you are sincerely interested in offering your support, you will quickly gain their approval, and they will include you in additional activities.

Charitable work offers you a chance to contribute to worthy causes and network and attract prospective collectors. Knowing what successful artists are doing in your area and where they network can help you determine where you might get some exposure of your own. Here are some examples of artists who have found a way to unite their creative talent with volunteerism and charity work for meaningful causes:

- Susan is a wildlife artist who contributes her work to many regional and national organizations, whose aims are to help save our planet, and raise the awareness of the catastrophic destruction that we are all causing.
- Jim, a sculptor, offered a special fund-raising exhibition to an organization for the blind. What a rewarding experience it was for him to share his art that the blind could see with their hands!
- Nadine created the poster for a high profile celebrity AIDS auction, which they sold as a limited edition print. In addition to the recognition she received, she immediately added a number of celebrities to her list of collectors!
- Kevin contributes his time and talent to a children's hospital in Kentucky. His drawings have been reproduced on note cards and posters which have helped to raise funds for the clinic. The

exposure he has received has led to exhibitions and sales. His humanitarian spirit has attracted others of the same nature. New friendships, which are rich in generosity and sharing, have resulted.

- Pierre regularly allocates proceeds from all sales to different local charities. Often the charity will publish news of his benevolent gesture in their bulletin or send out press releases on his behalf. Members of the press cover charity events more frequently than the run of the mill exhibition.
- Rolf's brightly-colored paintings depict social concerns in a whimsical style. He approached the Arthur Ashe Foundation and offered to get involved. They used his images on T-shirts and posters, which received world-wide television exposure.

> *If you want to lift yourself up,*
> *lift up someone else.*
> Booker T. Washington

Volunteerism is a great way to exercise and learn new skills, as well as develop self-esteem. As an artist, living in the suburbs, I volunteered my services regularly – presenting lectures and demonstrations and giving children free drawing lessons at the local library, organizing art events to raise funds for the Chamber of Commerce, and conducting creative discussion groups for patients at a psychiatric hospital. Those formative years helped me to develop many public relations skills: I grew from the knowledge I learned from working with other business professionals. When I arrived in New York, in 1980, having limited capital, and no professional resume, I volunteered to organize art exhibitions in community centers, banks, and night clubs. I offered to write art reviews in local community newspapers as an unpaid writer, which led to a paid position as an art critic for several art publications. As a member of New York Artists Equity Association, I served on the Board of Directors where I met the forerunners of art advocacy and helped to improve the state of the arts. When NYC Mayor David Dinkins asked me to participate as a juror on the Awards of Excellence in the Arts panel, I enjoyed contributing my time to this worthy cause. In recent years I have continued to jury exhibitions for non-profit organizations without being paid a fee. Every year I schedule several free workshops to reach artists who want to increase their education about the business of art.

You could say that volunteering has been a way of life for me. Over the years I have learned that from the beginning I was building up a positive reputation in the process of building those of others. The relationships with the artists, dealers, publishers and organizations that were planted several years ago have blossomed and continue to flourish today.

I don't need to emphasize the tremendous personal benefits that await the volunteer. To bring positive change to one's life and to be productive in our society, one must make time for meaningful pursuits – to help heal the world in the damaged places – even if it is a small contribution a step at a time.

When we grow old, there can only be one regret –
not to have given enough of ourselves.
Eleanora Duse

Chapter 14

The Art of Communication

*An artist cannot speak about his art
any more than
a plant can discuss horticulture.*
Jean Cocteau

The need to communicate is often a motivating factor in becoming an artist, but to succeed in the business community, the art of communication involves more than visual language. Verbal and written communication tools are necessary in the development of relationships and the preparation of important documents – correspondence, proposals, artist's statements, resumes and press releases.

Communication skills are necessary to develop a rapport and a mutually rewarding relationship with dealers, critics, curators and collectors.

Communication skills are required if you want to succeed at networking. It will require some desire and practice, until you feel at ease in this arena. When you attend an event, muster up the courage and make the effort to meet people. Behave in an approachable and friendly manner by smiling and laughing often. Speak with enthusiasm and confidence in order to arouse interest.

> *My method is to take the utmost trouble to find the right thing to say, and then to say it with the utmost levity.*
> George Bernard Shaw

In the course of your career, you will have to make many phone calls – to dealers, art suppliers, consultants and the press. Before you make the phone call, be prepared with a list of questions and topics of concern. Get into the right frame of mind. Focus. Prepare a brief introduction that immediately communicates the purpose of your call. Be considerate of the person's time, especially writers on deadlines. Avoid calling too early, too late and at lunch time. Stand up while speaking on the phone if you want to increase your energy level. Smile while you are speaking. Speak clearly and succinctly. Always act professionally, appropriately and in control.

At art receptions, social and business functions, you will be making new acquaintances who will want to know more about your work. Learn how to discuss the idea, content and motivation behind your work. Prepare a brief description of your work in a few short sentences, using words that create a picture – but do not sound rehearsed. Speak with enthusiasm.

When artist Roslyn Rose discusses her work she says: "I was inspired to create my current Assemblages by a desire to honor the histories and myths about women. As I continued to study this theme, I became intrigued with the lives of female artists who had died before their full potential was realized. I gather articles and ideas for my mixed media works during my foreign travels, visits to flea markets, and by collecting the cast-offs of friends and relatives."

Louis Mendez says: "My recent sculptural forms have explored the mystery and power of large monolithic heads, figures and torsos. Originally inspired by Olmec, Easter Island and Stonehenge rock carvings and arrangements, these works have grown into a highly personal expression of the struggle between the internal and external forces shaping the human condition."

Joan Giordano uses these words to describe her work: "These pieces emerge from singular cumulative experiences: the vast expanse of ocean, brilliant moss-green fungus, peeling tree bark, skins, crumbling walls and decay. My journey takes me deep into the earth to some ancient place within myself: inner reality becomes outer form. I am interested in the transformative nature of time – its relationship to materiality and to the evolution of form."

Many problems arise from not discussing our needs and feelings with others. Too often, we make abstruse remarks, expecting the other person to read our mind. Communicating verbally is a skill that requires practice. Think before your speak. Learn the art of clarification and repetition. Ask others to do the same. Ask for what you want and be direct, but temper your message with a regard for other's feelings and focus on obtaining positive results for all concerned.

One way in which a lack of communication becomes a problem is when it threatens a relationship between the artist and his or her dealer. Exercise the ability to discuss questions and concerns relating to what is expected from each other. Conflicting opinions need to be resolved, and compromises need to be made, but the problems can only be solved through discussion.

Did you know that most of our communication is *non*-verbal? Beyond the words, themselves, is a host of clues as to what the speaker is communicating. Beware of what you may be communicating through your body posture and movement, facial expression, position of hands, your handshake, eye contact and voice tone. You want to be sure that what you are saying verbally is consistent with your body language – genuine and self-assured.

We teach people how to treat us. If we are being treated badly, perhaps it is something we are communicating that is the cause. Look for the subtle ways – especially in your body language and voice tonality, as well as the choice of words, in which you may be relaying messages of insecurity, vulnerability or low self-esteem.

It is important to express gratitude to those who have contributed in some way to your success, however small or grand the gesture. Much of your success is dependent upon what others do for you. If you make it a pleasant experience and show appreciation they will look forward to repeating it. Many meaningful professional relationships are lost to artists because they fail to exercise etiquette. That includes thanking individuals who attended your exhibitions, writers who mention your work in an article and friends and associates who recommend your work for a commission or you for a position.

> *Writing is easy.*
> *All you have to do*
> *is stare at a blank sheet of paper*
> *until drops of blood form on your forehead.*
> Gene Fowler

That which we are capable of feeling,
we are capable of saying.
Miguel de Cervantes

The Power of Keeping a Journal

A journal is a powerful tool to enhance your dialogue, because it requires absorbing communication with yourself. As you write a few thoughts each day, your ideas about what is important, your mission and your goals, will become crystal clear. You'll automatically discover and reaffirm what you really want in life. The process of writing in a journal is a form of meditation. It has a similar power to quiet the mind and focus your thoughts. It provides ventilation for the annoying chatter.

A journal affirms the reality of your life. Writing about life adds meaning. Writing about your first solo show, your first major corporate sale or a creative breakthrough will balance your spirits the next time you're feeling low. Writing about your creative conflicts will help you move through them. Writing about your pain will help you to heal.

A journal helps you speak out. Many of your notes will become important parts of your artist's statement. Ideas and feelings form into words which grow into sentences and paragraphs, until they create the need for a forum in which to express themselves.

Over time, your journal will reveal the reoccurring obstacles and stress points in your life. As you start to acknowledge them, they will lose their control over you, and you begin the journey to overcome them. The tools you gain will help you to solve the issues that surface in the process of making your art. The challenges of shaping, balancing, composing, structuring, releasing, beginning and completing will flow more freely.

Art Heals
From My Journal, July 30, 1996

Art heals. Art heals. We've heard it a million times. It's become a catch phrase in the 90s. I've punctuated it, emphasized it and proclaimed it in my workshops on empowerment and in my consultations – to motivate artists and emphasize its significance.

I don't think I've ever before known the true meaning of the words. Lately, those words have had a profound impact on me. They have reached out to me, embraced me, and wrapped themselves around me in a cloak of great comfort and consolation.

During the past two years death and mortality have stared at me defiantly and, in a relentless, in-your-face manner. My sister had a mastectomy. I waited in a hospital for six long hours during her surgery. I watched her endure chemotherapy and radiation treatments. After her ordeal, they discovered more "spots" and recommend more surgery and chemotherapy. Whenever I think about those spots, they appear in my mind like huge, black dots racing toward me from a Lichtenstein painting. The thought of her fear and suffering constricts my heart, almost paralyzing me. The idea of losing her – my dear sister – leaves a black void in my soul. The idea of her two young sons without their loving mother is incomprehensible.

At the same time, I am gradually losing my mother. Physically, she is healthy; but her mind is slowly deteriorating. She forgets. Events, days of the week, frequently, entire conversations. Her memories are slowly fading. She telephones me several times a day to find out the date, desperately reaching out for comfort during her bleak, terrifying loneliness.

I noticed recently that I receive comfort from the images that surround me. During a stressful and frustrating conversation with my mother, I look at the eloquent, fluid lines of a beautiful abstract sculpture that evokes the human form. It brings me peace. The colors undulate and modify their shapes against the cool light reflected from my window. What seems like eternity, I become one with the art, escaping into the shapes of the solid wood that defines and alters negative space. The turmoil dissipates during my visual exploration, and the healing process is subtle. Sometimes, my eyes will embrace the soothing affects of the beauty of art before it registers in my brain.

I recall countless instances at the computer when my gaze drifted above the screen and focused on a Japanese woodblock print – how it helped me to focus and bring things into perspective. Suddenly, the screen, that had been blank, started to fill up with words that rolled off my fingertips. The vision before me of the ceremonious Japanese women, gently wrapped in their kimonos, seemed to whisper in a form of haiku chant: "Be still, relax, a fountain of words will flow from you..." These images have carried me through many important deadlines.

Every morning I walk into my office and one of the first things I see is my Chinese rug made with loving hands. It is gently patterned with lotus blossoms and leaves in colors of sepia, beige and yellow, and it appears as though I am looking into a sea of endless possibilities. Only recently did I become aware of this daily ritual and the secret power it has bestowed.

Much of my time is spent on the phone speaking to artists from around the world. I often sit on my couch as I speak, and allow a brightly colored photo montage to soothe my soul. This gift from an artist, with its purples, yellows, reds and greens complement each other, striking a balance and harmony. Its translucent forms that overlap, merge and shift will hold my interest for long periods of time. The shapes that stand alone and, yet, gracefully intertwine symbolize the connection I've established with artists and, at the same time, the respect I have for their individuality. The constant flux I see in the art reminds me to keep an open mind to different people's views.

Nature also restores my energy. As I look out my window at the ever-changing shapes of clouds and birds flying high above the city's rooftops I feel a sense of freedom and space. However, the special relationship I have with art is quite different. On a deeper level, I am aware that it was created by human hands. Sensing the experiences and feelings of an artist enhances my life. For me it represents a part of history and expresses the endurance of humanity. The best and most restorative part of my relationship with art that surrounds me, is the way it touches my subconscious and fortifies me. I am deeply grateful to artists everywhere for their loving devotion to the creative process and their power to heal.

I am propelled to reach for a canvas more often lately. Whether I spend a few hours or an entire day immersed in the wonders of creation without caring about the results, I know that many of my moments would seem unbearable and exasperating without it. Art helps me to survive the most difficult challenges, and therefore, art most certainly heals.

APPENDIX 1

80 Mantras For Success
I will...

1. Define success in my own terms.
2. Rejoice that I am an artist.
3. Celebrate my unique vision.
4. Nurture my creativity.
5. Strive to reach my potential.
6. Refuse to be afraid of rejection.
7. Ignore destructive criticism.
8. Learn from constructive criticism.
9. Avoid toxic materials and toxic relationships.
10. Take responsibility for my career.
11. Strive to achieve self-sufficiency.
12. Get my priorities straight and keep on course.
13. Find the root of my passion, values and life's mission.
14. Live my life with passion.
15. Take positive action daily.
16. Seize the opportunity to learn from every misfortune.
17. Build strong relationships in the art community.
18. Have the courage to set and accomplish high goals.
19. Set three sets of goals: artistic; career; and financial.
20. Create excellent quality promotional/sales materials.
21. Increase my knowledge about the business of art.
22. Talk about my art with clarity and enthusiasm.
23. Exude confidence, even if I have to fake it at times.
24. Be committed to building a strong body of work.
25. Continue to grow and groom my mailing list.
26. Contribute time and effort to improve the status of artists.
27. Make my work visible and accessible on an on-going basis.
28. Exercise diversity in creating and exhibiting my work.
29. Circulate visual "handouts" of my work routinely and persistently.
30. Devise a marketing plan and break it down into monthly, weekly, and daily activities.
31. Stress the benefits of my art to prospective buyers.
32. Contact at least two people each day for business growth.
33. Follow up and follow through.
34. Improve at least one aspect of my career every day.
35. Keep my resume and other materials updated.

36. Learn the art of polite, yet assertive, self-promotion.
37. Copyright my work.
38. Investigate gallery owners/agents before beginning a relationship.
39. Protect my integrity and my art.
40. Not wait for my art to sell itself.
41. Express enthusiasm about my work to everyone I meet.
42. Allow others own my work.
43. Exercise a positive perception about selling.
44. Stop procrastinating *Now!*
45. Reject the myth "the poor starving artist."
46. Develop a healthy partnership with money.
47. Get a grip on my cash flow.
48. Make use of "green power."
49. Exercise generosity.
50. Exchange support with a network of artists.
51. Share my contacts and information freely with other artists.
52. Take time to celebrate every one of my accomplishments.
53. Always be prepared for success.
54. Avoid galleries that charge artists to exhibit their work.
55. Never leave my art work anywhere without a written consignment agreement.
56. Always use a signed, written contract with a gallery.
57. Never submit poor quality presentation materials, under any circumstances.
58. Never lie on my resume.
59. Use my resume as a sales tool and keep it growing.
60. Avoid over-pricing my work.
61. Refuse to under-value my work.
62. Never sell my work at bargain prices from my studio.
63. Become a proficient *Artrepreneur*.
64. Practice the "rule of thirds."
65. Get out of my studio and participate in life.
66. Express appreciation to those who help my career.
67. Get help from human and technological resources.
68. Sell to and, buy from, fellow artists.
69. View professional success as a journey, not a destination.
70. Exercise commitment to my art and my career.
71. Share my vision with collectors and fellow artists.
72. Be a good listener; avoid the need to hear myself speak.
73. Keep on top of art events and trends.
74. Be receptive to change.
75. Not burn any bridges.
76. Never give up – ever!
77. Employ the motivational assistance of coaches and the teachings of mentors.
78. Be flexible. When one plan fails, try another.
79. Not rely on one source of power.
80. Not wait to be discovered. I will make it happen!

APPENDIX 2

Selected Artists' Groups, Arts Organizations, Councils and Foundations

ADVERTISING PHOTOGRAPHERS OF AMERICA (APA), 333 South Beverly Drive, Beverly Hills, CA 90212. Promotes high professional standards and ethics. Communicates and exchanges information among APA chapters.

ADVERTISING PHOTOGRAPHERS OF NEW YORK (APNY), 27 West 20 St., New York, NY 10010. A professional trade association that promotes the highest standards of business practice within the industry. Publishes APNY Newsletter and operates APNY Hotline.

THE ALLIANCE OF ARTISTS' COMMUNITIES, 2311 East Burnside, Portland, Oregon 97214. Tel: (503) 797-6988. Fax: (503) 797-9560. Email: aac@teleport.com. A national service organization that supports the field of artists' communities and residency programs. Encourages collaboration among members of the field, provides leadership on field issues, raises the visibility of artists' communities, promotes philanthropy in the field, and generally encourages programs that support the creation of art. Composed of about 55 leading, nonprofit artists' communities and 40 individuals. Continues to accept new members who provide artists with time, space, facilities, and a community environment in which to create their work. Publishes the *Artists' Communities Directory.*

ALLIANCE FOR THE ARTS, 330 West 42nd Street, New York, NY 10036. Tel: (212) 947-6340. Fax: (212) 947-6416. Dedicated to policy research, information services and advocacy for the arts in New York. Has influenced the policies and actions of government, funders, and the business of art. Gathers and analyzes data about the arts in New York, identifying the needs, contributions, and issues facing members of the artistic community.

ALLIANCE OF QUEENS ARTISTS (AQA), 99-10 Metropolitan Ave., Forest Hills, NY 11375. Tel: (718) 520-9842. Executive Director: Bob Menzel. A membership organization for artists who live in the New York metropolitan area. Fosters and promotes the visual arts through exhibitions and other activities.

AMERICAN ABSTRACT ARTISTS, 470 West End Ave., #9D, New York, NY 10024. President: Beatrice Riese. Promotes American Abstract art by bringing it before the public, and fostering public appreciation of this direction in painting and sculpture. Affords artists an opportunity for developing their own work by providing forums for the exchange of ideas among themselves.

THE AMERICAN ACADEMY IN ROME, 7 East 60 Street, New York, NY 10022. Tel: (212) 751-7200. Fax: (212) 751-7220. http:// www. aarome.org. The only American overseas center for independent study and advanced research in the fine arts and the humanities. Annual Rome Prize fellowship program supports twenty-six individuals working in archaeology, architecture, classical studies, design arts, historic preservation and conservation, history of art, landscape architecture, post-classical humanistic studies and visual arts.

AMERICAN ARTISTS PROFESSIONAL LEAGUE, (AAPL), C/O Salmagundi Club, 47 Fifth Ave., New York, NY 10003. Tel: (212) 645-1345. The country's authority on artist's pigments and works to set the standards for pigments and artists materials. Protects artists' interests and traditional realism in American Art.

THE AMERICAN CERAMIC SOCIETY, P.O. Box 6136, Westerville, OH 43086. Tel: (614) 890-4700. Fax: (614) 899-6109. Email: info@acers.org. URL:http://www.acers.org The world's leading organization dedicated to the advancement of ceramics. Provides the latest technical, scientific and educational information to its members and others in the ceramics and related materials field, and the general public.

AMERICAN CRAFT COUNCIL, 72 Spring, Street, New York, NY 10012. Tel: (212) 274-0630. Conducts juried shows and offers group rates on insurance. Co-publisher of *The Voice,* a bimonthly newsletter. Operates a slide registry on American craft artists in all media.

THE AMERICAN FEDERATION OF ARTS (AFA), 41 East 65 St., New York, NY 10021. Tel: (212) 988-7700. Fax: (212) 861-2487. The nation's oldest and most comprehensive museum service organization. Strengthens the ability of museums to enrich the public's experience and understanding of art. Presents traveling art exhibitions of AFA member institutions and helps institutions that are interested in organizing and circulating fine arts exhibitions to other museums.

AMERICAN INSTITUTE OF GRAPHIC ARTS, 164 Fifth Avenue New York, NY 10010. Tel: (212) 807-1990. URL: http://www.aiga.org. Promotes graphic design in books and other media, through exhibitions, seminars, journals, and publications. 38 chapters nationally.

AMERICAN INSTITUTE OF ARCHITECTS (AIA), New York Chapter, 200 Lexington Ave., New York, NY 10016. Tel: (212) 683-0023. Fax: (212) 696-5022. URL: http://www.aiany.org. Provides a wide range of educational programs open both to members and the general public.

AMERICAN RENAISANCE FOR THE TWENTY-FIRST CENTURY (ART), F.D.R. Station, PO Box 8379, NY, NY 10150. Tel: (212) 759-7765. Fax: (212) 759-1922. President: Alexandra York. Promotes and advances public knowledge and understanding of Western heritage art forms. Gives grants to artists. Exhibits new and experimental as well as traditional works of art. Presents educational programs, lecture series, and special events. Publishes *ART ideas* magazine.

AMERICAN SOCIETY OF ARTISTS, INC., PO Box 1326, Palatine, IL 60078 (312) 751-2500; (847) 991-4748. A national organization that presents art and craft shows, lectures, and demonstrations. Publishes *Artisan* a quarterly newsletter.

AMERICAN SOCIETY OF CONTEMPORARY ARTISTS, (ASCA), C/O Joseph Lubrano, President, 130 Gale Place, 9-H, Bronx, NY 10463. Tel: (718) 548-6790. Represents, through exhibitions of its members, the varied currents of 20th century art, in galleries and alternative spaces.

AMERICAN SOCIETY OF MEDIA PHOTOGRAPHERS (ASMP) National, 14 Washington Road, Suite 502 Princetonjunction, NJ 08550. Tel: (609) 799-8300. Other national chapters. A trade organization for print and electronic photographers.

AMERICAN WATERCOLOR SOCIETY, C/O Salmagundi Club, 47 Fifth Ave., NY, NY 10003. Tel: (212) 206-8986. Oldest and largest watercolor society. Advances watercolor painting, awards scholarships, holds demonstrations and a national watercolor exhibition, and exchanges exhibitions with other countries.

AMERICANS FOR THE ARTS, One East 53 St., New York, NY 10022. Tel: (212) 223-2787. Fax: (212) 980-4857. Works with cultural organizations, arts and business leaders and patrons to provide leadership, advocacy, visibility, professional development, research and information to advance support for the arts and culture in our nation's communities.

APERTURE FOUNDATION, 20 East 23 St. New York, NY 10010. Tel: (212) 505-5555. Fax: (212) 979-7759. Non-profit publisher of photography related books and periodicals.

ART DEALERS ASSOCIATION OF AMERICA (ADAA), 575 Madison Ave., New York, NY 10022. Tel: (212) 940-8590. Fax: (212) 940-7013. URL: http:// www.artdealers. org. An organization of the nation's leading fine art dealers. Promotes the highest standards of connoiseurship, scholarship, and ethical practice within the profession and increases public awareness of the role and responsibilities of reputable art dealers. Sponsors "The Art Show," an annual exhibition of leading American galleries at The Seventh Regiment Armory, in NYC.

ART GROUP FOR LESBIAN AND GAY ARTISTS, PO Box 1515 Cooper Station, New York, NY 10276. Tel: (212) 473-7130. Provides motivation, support, and networking possibilities for its members. Seeks and creates exhibition opportunities to show the work of lesbian and gay artists. Publishes a newsletter for its members.

ART IN EMBASSIES PROGRAM, U.S. Dept. of State, A/Art, Room B258, Washington DC, 20520. Tel: (202) 647-5723. Fax: (202) 647-4080. Offers artists the opportunity to have their work exhibited worldwide, by lending their art to embassies.

THE ART INFORMATION CENTER, Director Dan Concholar, 55 Mercer St., New York, NY 10012. Tel: (212) 966-3443. Advises artists on New York gallery system and suggests appropriate galleries for their work.

ART IN GENERAL, 79 Walker Street, New York, NY 10013. Tel: (212) 219-0473. Email: info@artingeneral.org. URL:http:// www/artingeneral.org. Alternative exhibition space that shows all styles and media including video and installations, primarily group thematic exhibitions. Panel of 10 artists reviews work on quarterly basis. Pays honorarium to artists.

ARTIST'S ALLIANCE OF CALIFORNIA, P.O. Box 2424 Nevada City, CA 95959. Tel: (916) 272-7357. Members receive discounts on art materials, health insurance, discounted legal and accounting services, museum memberships, travel services and a newsletter.

THE ARTISTS COMMUNITY FEDERAL CREDIT UNION, 155 Avenue of the Americas, 14th floor, New York, NY 10013. Federally insured credit union that provides services to assist artists in establishing a credit rating.

ARTISTS SPACE, 38 Greene Street, Third Floor, New York, NY 10013. Tel: (212) 226-3970. Fax: (212) 966-1434. A pioneer in alternative spaces. Supports contemporary art by exhibiting emerging artists in fine art, video, performance, architecture, and design. Encourages diversity and experimentation. Maintains a computerized Artists File, accessible to artists, curators and the public.

ARTISTS FOR ART, 514 Lackawanna Avenue, Scranton, PA 18503. A membership organization of artists and supporters of the Arts. Fosters an appreciation of the visual arts, by presenting it to the Northeastern Pennsylvania region. AFA Gallery is a venue for regional artists and artists from outside this region.

ARTISTS TALK ON ART, (ATOA), C/O Phoenix Gallery, 568 Broadway, Suite #607,10012. Tel: (212) 226-8711. Executive Director: Donna Marxer. Organizes panels discussions on current and vital art issues led by prominent art professionals.

ARTS COUNCIL OF THE MORRIS AREA, PO Box 370, Madison, NJ 07940. Tel: (973) 377-6622. Fax: (973) 301-2040. Promotes the arts through education, information, support and promotion of all disciplines of artistic expression.

ARTTABLE, INC., 270 Lafayette St., Suite 608, New York, NY 10012. Tel: (212) 343-1735.Fax: (212) 343-1430. A national organization for professional women in the visual arts. Fosters and promotes greater understanding and appreciation of the visual arts by providing a forum for the exchange of ideas and information through educational programs and events for its members and the general public.

ASSOCIATION OF HISPANIC ARTS, INC., 250 West 26 Street, 4th floor, 10001. Tel: (212) 727-7227. A Latino arts-service organization serving primarily New York with information, technical help, workshops and seminars. Publishes the *AHA Hispanic Arts News,* the *Directory of Hispanic Artists and Organizations.*

ATLANTIC CENTER FOR THE ARTS (ACA), 1414 Art Center Ave., New Smyrna Beach, FL 32168. Tel: (904) 427-6975. Fax (904) 427-5669. Nonprofit, interdisciplinary artists-in-residence community and arts education facility dedicated to promoting artistic excellence by providing talented artists an opportunity to work and collaborate with some of the world's most distinguished contemporary artists in the fields of composing, visual, literary and performing arts. Community interaction is coordinated through on-site and outreach presentations, performances and exhibitions.

BRONX COUNCIL ON THE ARTS, 1738 Hone Ave., Bronx, NY 10461. Tel: (718) 931-9500. The officially designated arts council of the Bronx. Provides exhibitions at the Longwood Gallery, 965 Longwood Ave., Bronx 10459. Tel: (718) 842-5659. Presents business workshops for artists.

BRONX RIVER ART CENTER, 1087 East Tremont Ave., Bronx, 10460. Tel: (718) 589-5819 and (718) 589-6379. A place where artists, both emerging and established, can create and exhibit their works. A forum where new, experimental, and provocative ideas can be explored and presented for public debate.

BROOKLYN WATERCOLOR SOCIETY, C/O Joseph Lubrano, President, 130 Gale Place, 9-H, Bronx, NY 10463. Tel: (718) 548-6790. Non-sectarian organization of juried artists shares ideas and encourages interest in the transparent watercolor medium, through critiques and exhibitions. Through its Awards Fund donates cash awards to a deserving Brooklyn-affiliated arts institution, art group, or talented art student.

BURR ARTISTS, C/O Fred Schwartz, President, 325 West 86th St., #12B, New York, NY 10024. Exhibits members' work of varied styles and media in a range of alternative exhibition venues throughout NYC.

THE BUSINESS COMMITTEE FOR THE ARTS (BCA), 1775 Broadway, Suite 510, New York, NY 10019.Tel: (212) 664-0600.Fax: (212) 956-5980. Fosters business/arts alliances through research, publications, seminars and conferences. Provides individualized consultations to guide companies in their investments in the arts. Reports on issues and trends in business-arts alliances.

THE CALIFORNIA WATERCOLOR ASSOCIATION (CWA), P.O. Box 4631, Walnut Creek, CA 94598. Tel: (925) 648-9113. Largest regional watermedia organization in California dedicated to the artistic growth of artists of all ages. Provides scholarship funds to students to help further their study of art. Gives merchandise awards, cash and gift certificates to deserving students and to art community projects. Sponsors an art exhibition for a high school district. Its outreach program includes visitations to schools to help stimulate the growth of art.

CENTER FOR BOOK ARTS, 626 Broadway, 5th floor, 10012. Tel: (212) 460-9768. Fax: (212) 673-4635. Email: bookarts@ pipeline. com. URL:http://www. colophon. com. Preserves traditional crafts of bookmaking, as well as contemporary interpretations of the book as an art object. Ensures that the ancient craft of the book, that container which preserves the knowledge and ideas of a culture, remains a viable and vital part of our civilization. Exhibits traditional and contemporary, one-of-a-kind and limited edition, artists books, in all media.

CHICAGO ARTISTS' COALITION, 11East Hubbard Street, 7th Floor Chicago, IL 60611. Tel: (312) 670-2060. Artist-run multi-cultural coalition of visual artists and friends, brought together to fulfill four basic needs: education, advocacy, provision of professional and education services and the improvement of the artist's living environment. Publishes *The Chicago Artists' News,* a monthly newsletter, and other resource books.

CITYARTS, INC. 525 Broadway, Suite 700 New York, NY 10012. Tel: (212) 966-0377. Email: info@ cityarts.org. URL: http://www. cityarts.org. Dedicated to creating public art of the highest caliber in communities where access to and participation in the arts are limited. Brings professional artists together with the youth of these neighborhoods to design and create murals, mosaics, sculptures, and other forms of art, serving to transform desolate and forgotten walls into vibrant public spaces. Artists may obtain an Artist Application from its website or request one by fax, postal mail, or email.

COLLEGE ART ASSOCIATION OF AMERICA, 275 Seventh Ave., New York, NY 10001.Tel: (212) 691-1051. Fax: (212) 627-2381. Email: Nyoffice@collegeart.org. URL:http://www.collegeat.org. Promotes and enhances excellence in the practice and teaching aspects of art and art history. Holds an annual conference. Maintains a career placement service, group medical and life insurance. Publishes *Art Bulletin* and *Artjoumal* and *CAA Careers*, which lists college and museum art jobs.

CREATIVE TIME, 307 Seventh Ave., #1904., New York, NY 10001. Tel: (212) 206-6674. Fax: (212) 255-8467. URL: http://www. creative time.org. Presents writers, visual artists, choreographers, musicians, architects, video and filmmakers who cross disciplines, reinvent forms, rescue neglected sites, participate in unusual collaborations, investigate cultural influences, confront social issues and encourage public dialogue.

DIVERSEWORKS, 1117 East Freeway, Houston, TX 77000. Tel: (713) 223-8346. URL:http:// www. diverseworks.org. Dedicated to presenting new visual, performing, and literary art. Encourages the investigation of current artistic, cultural and social issues. Builds, educates, and sustains audiences for contemporary art.

ELIZABETH FOUNDATION FOR THE ARTS, PO Box 2670, New York, NY 10108. Fax: (212) 586-5896. Email: grants@efa1.org. Awards twelve to fifteen grants each year to assist artists in creating new work and / or gaining recognition for their work. Selection is based on work presented in slides, demonstrated financial need, background and dedication to career and proposal for use of grant. Application forms and guidelines, available by sending an informal written request by mail, fax or email.

EN FOCO, INC., 32 E. Kingsbridge Rd., Bronx, NY 10468. Tel/Fax: (718) 584-7718. Email: Enfocoinc @aol.com. Dedicated to producing exhibitions, publications and events which support culturally diverse photographers and brings their work to a larger audience. Touring Gallery Program presents photographic exhibitions in public spaces in NYC and NY state.

EXIT ART/THE FIRST WORLD, 548 Broadway, 10012. Tel: (212) 966-7745. Fax: (212) 925-2928. Email: exitart@interport.net. URL: http://www. exitart.org. Dedicated to transcultural, multi-disciplinary explorations of contemporary art issues. Organizes and presents experimental and historical projects exploring the diversity of contemporary culture in the visual arts, theater, design, film and video. Exhibits contemporary art in all media including performance and multimedia.

FLUSHING COUNCIL ON CULTURE & THE ARTS, INC., 137-35 Northern Blvd., Flushing, NY 11354. Lucy Davidson, Director of Art Services:

Tel: (718) 463-7700, extension 228. Email: Lucydfcca @aol.com. Promotes the arts as a way of bridging cultural understanding among all people. Provides ongoing programs in the performing and visual arts to residents and visitors.

THE FOUNDATION CENTER, 79 Fifth Ave., New York, NY 10003. Tel: (212) 620-4230. URL:http:// www.fdncenter.org. Resource center for information about funding opportunities. Provides complete information on philanthropic support of the arts and other areas, private and public grant, loan and fellowship opportunities.

GEN ART, Art of The Next Generation, 145 West 28 St., #11C, New York, NY 10001.Tel: (212) 290-0312. Fax: (212) 290-0254. URL: http://www.genart.org. Exposes the works of young emerging artists, filmmakers, fashion designers, and members of the industry and the community at large. Curates group shows and offers consultations for collectors.

ADOLPH AND ESTHER GOTTLIEB FOUNDATION, 380 W. Broadway, New York, NY 10012. Tel: (212) 226-0581. Fax: (212) 226-0584. Provides financial support to individual artists who have shown a lifetime of commitment to their art. Emergency Assistance Program for a specific emergency, such as fire, flood, or emergency medical need.

GRAPHIC ARTISTS GUILD, 90 John Street, Suite 403, New York, NY 10038. Tel: (212) 791-3400. Fax (212) 791-0333. URL: http://www.gag.org. President: Polly M. Law. Promotes and protects the economic interests of its members. Improves conditions for all creators of graphic art, and raises standards for the entire industry. Publisher of pricing guidelines for manual and digital art and *Guild News: The Graphic Artists Guild National Newsletter.*

THE ELIZABETH GREENSHIELDS FOUNDATION, 1814 Sherbrooke West, Ste. 1, Montreal, Quebec, Canada H3H 1E4. Tel: (514) 937-9225. Fax: (514) 937-0141. Gives grants to young artists of all nationalities in the early stages of their careers, in painting, drawing, printmaking, and sculpture. Work must be representational or figurative. Candidates are required to have already started or completed training in an established school of art, and/or demonstrate, through past work and future plans, a commitment to making art a lifetime career.

JOHN SIMON GUGGENHEIM MEMORIAL FOUNDATION, Art Department, Scholarship/Grant Program, 90 Park Ave., New York, NY 10016. Tel: (212) 687-4470 Fax: (212) 697-3248. Offers fellowships to further the development of scholars and artists by assisting them to engage in research in any field of knowledge and creation in any of the arts, under the freest possible conditions and irrespective of race, color, or creed.

HENRY STREET SETTLEMENT, ABRONS ART CENTER, 466 Grand St., New York, NY 10002. Tel: (212) 598-0400. Fax: (212) 505-8329. URL:http://www. artground. com/ henrystva.htm. Exhibits emerging, women and artists of color. Artist-in-Residence work space program (artists may send SASE for application), an Arts-in-Education program (workshops by professional artists and arts educators are implemented in classrooms from pre-kindergarten through high school), and a gallery education program. Presents artists' talks and symposiums.

THE ILLINOIS ARTS COUNCIL, State of Illinois Center, 100 West Randolph, Suite 10-500, Chicago, IL 60601. Tel: (312) 814-6750. 800-237-6994. Maintains the Illinois Artists Registry, a computerized mailing list service designed as a comprehensive directory to link artists with professional opportunities. Contains up-to-date information about participating Illinois artists.

INTERNATIONAL FESTIVALS AND EXHIBITIONS FUND FOR U.S. ARTISTS, Arts International, United Nations Plaza, New York, NY 10017. Tel: (212) 984-5370. Awards grants from $500-$25,000 to individuals and groups invited to perform at festivals or curate exhibitions overseas.

INTERNATIONAL SCULPTURE CENTER, 1050 17th Street NW, Suite 250 Washington, DC 20036. Tel: (202) 785-1144. Fax: (202) 785-0810. ISC Business Office: 401 N. Michigan Ave., Suite 2200, Chicago, IL 60611. Tel: (312) 527-6634. A membership organization founded to advance the creation and understanding of sculpture and its unique and vital contribution to society. Biennial conference gathers over 1,000 sculpture enthusiasts to network and dialogue about technical, aesthetic, and professional issues. Offers membership discounts. Publishes *Sculpture* magazine. Members include sculptors, collectors, architects, developers, journalists, curators, historians, critics, educators, foundries, galleries, museums.

MATTRESS FACTORY, 500 Sampsonia Way, Pittsburgh, PA 15212-4444. Tel: (412) 231-3169. Fax: (412)322-2231. Email: info@ mattress. org. URL:http:// www. mattress.org. A research and development lab for artists and a museum of contemporary art. Commissions, exhibits, and collects site-specific installations. Education program emphasizes creative process and its positive effect on problem-solving in daily life and other academic areas.

MIDATLANTIC ARTS, 22 Light Street, Suite 300, Baltimore, MD 21202. URL:http:// www. charm.

APPENDIX 2

net/~midarts. Program Assistant, Artists' Programs and Panel Operations: Jacque Gourley: jacque@midarts.usa.com. Provides leadership to artists and arts organizations in DE, District of Columbia, MD, NJ, NY, PA, VA, U.S. VI, and West VA. Encourages continued development of the arts supports arts programs throughout the region, the nation and the world.

THE MILLAY COLONY FOR THE ARTS, INC., 444 East Hill Rd., PO Box 3, Austerlitz, NY 12017 Tel: (518) 392-3103. Email: @millaycolony.org. URL: http: // www.millaycolony.org. Artist-in-residence program. Provides one month residencies to painters, collagists, sculptors, photographers, novelists, poets, nonfiction writers, biographers, playwrights, screenwriters, performance artists, and composers. Designed to accommodate creativity. Gives artists private studio and separate living quarters.

NATIONAL ARTISTS EQUITY ASSOCIATION, INC., PO Box 28068, Central Station, Washington, DC 20005. Tel: (202) 628-9633. Advocacy organization for visual artists, with branches throughout the U.S. Publishes a newsletter, and offers health insurance, business and legal assistance.

NATIONAL ARTS CLUB, 15 Gramercy Park South, 10003. Tel: (212) 475-3424. Fax: (212) 475-3692. A private club that supports and embraces all of the arts disciplines. Presents exhibitions in three gallery spaces.

NATIONAL ASSOCIATION OF ARTISTS' ORGANIZATIONS, 918 F Street, NW, Washington, DC 20004. A membership organization consisting of organizations and individual artists. Provides information on legislative issues and government policies affecting artists and art organizations.

NATIONAL ASSOCIATION OF WOMEN ARTISTS (NAWA), 41 Union Square West, #906, New York, NY 10003. Tel: (212) 675-1616. A non-political, member supported organization. The oldest and largest woman artists exhibiting organization. Encourages and promotes the creative output of women artists while seeking exhibition spaces for its members.

NEW ENGLAND FOUNDATION FOR THE ARTS, 330 Congress Street 6th Floor Boston MA 02215 Tel: (617) 951 0010. Fax: (617) 951 0016. URL:http://www.nefa.org. Connects the people of New England with the power of art to shape our lives and improve our communities. Programs support artists and presenters in the visual and performing arts. Shares information and technology to expand and enrich the arts infrastructure. Strengthens the role of the arts in building communities.

NEW YORK ARTISTS EQUITY ASSOCIATION, 498 Broome St., New York, NY 10013. Tel: (212) 941-0130. URL: http://www. anny. org. Disseminates information regarding legislation and legal rights, all in the interest of effectively addressing "survival" issues relevant to artists. Monitors local, state and federal legislation and strongly advocates bills in support of art and artists. Protects the legal rights of artists. Holds art-related panel discussions. Publishes *The Artist's Proof*, a quarterly newsletter available to its members. Maintains a street-level gallery, available for rent to individual artists, dealers and art groups.

NEW YORK CITY DEPARTMENT OF CULTURAL AFFAIRS, 330 West 42 St., 14th floor, New York, NY 10036. Tel: (212) 643-7770. Fax: (212) 643-7780. Helps to oversee, sustain and promote arts and culture in New York City. An advocacy agency, a source of funding and a major resource for many arts organizations. "Percent for Art" Program offers city agencies the opportunity to allocate 1% of the capital budget of eligible city construction projects for commissioning new art work and/or the conservation of existing public art.

NEW YORK FOUNDATION FOR THE ARTS, 155 Avenue of the Americas, New York, NY 10013. Tel: (212) 366-6900. Fax: (212) 366-1778. URL:http://www. artswire. org/nyfa/nyfa.htm. Fellowships, residencies, project support, loans, fiscal sponsorship of small to medium sized arts organizations, and information services for artists and organizations in all artistic areas in the U.S. Publishes *F.Y.I.*, a resource newsletter. Operates Visual Artists Hotline, a free information service for individual artists working in all visual arts media. Call (800) 232-2789 between 2-5 EST, Mon-Fri. Http:// www. nyfa.org/hotline_ newyorkcity.pdf

NEW YORK SOCIETY OF WOMEN ARTISTS. A membership organization of NYC area professional women artists. Provides venue for women to exhibit their work in a professional environment. Members juried in April. Two-dimensional artists contact Catchi, 2 Grist Mill Lane, Manhasset, NY 11030. Three-dimensional artists contact Janet Indick, 428 Sagamore Ave., Teaneck, NJ 07666.

NEW YORK STATE COUNCIL ON THE ARTS (NYSCA), 915 Broadway, New York, NY 10010.Tel: (212) 387-7000. Fax: (212) 387-7164. Promotes and develops New York's cultural, economic and human resources through support of the arts. Funds non-profit organizations to provide cultural services to NY state citizens. Awards a variety of grants in the performing and visual arts.

NORTHEAST WATERCOLOR SOCIETY, (NEWS) Membership contact: Matilda Grech, 93 E Main Street, Port Jervis, NY 12771. Promotes and preserves watercolor painting. Members consist of a wide range of artists including many of the most recognized artists in this medium. Annual October Juried Show open to all U.S. artists.

THE OHIO RIVER BORDER INITIATIVE (ORBI), www.orbi.org. A program that provides funding to a wide variety of projects, artists and community groups in West Virginia and Ohio counties that border the Ohio River. Grants are awarded for projects that actively involve artists, audiences and communities. Annual deadline is around February 1.

ORGANIZATION OF INDEPENDENT ARTISTS (O.I.A.), 19 Hudson St., Room 402, New York, NY 10013. Tel: (212) 219-9213. Fax: (212) 219-9216. Provides public spaces for exhibitions throughout New York and in its own gallery. Maintains a slide registry available to curators, art professionals, artists and others. Publishes a newsletter and conducts slide viewings. Conducts two annual Curators Workshops and one annual juried Salon Exhibition.

PASTEL SOCIETY, C/O National Arts Club, 15 Gramercy Park, New York, NY 10003. President: Sidney H. Hermel. Encourages the use of pastel, educates the public regarding the permanence and beauty of pastels, and offers workshops and classes as part of the education in the medium. Pastel artists of high quality in all styles are exhibited in shows with numerous awards.

PEN & BRUSH CLUB, 16 East 10 St., New York, NY 10003. Tel: (212) 475-3669. Fax: (212) 475-6018. The oldest organization of professional women in the arts in the U.S. Establishes high standards in the various arts disciplines. Stimulates and develops the professional activities of its members. Enriches cultural diversity of the neighborhood.

POLLACK-KRASNER FOUNDATION, 863 Park Ave., New York, NY 10021. Tel: (212) 517-5400. Fax: (212) 288-2836. Foundation Grant provides financial assistance to individual working artists of established ability. Offers financial assistance to artists of recognized merit and financial need working as painters, sculptors, mixed media and installation artists.

PROFESSIONAL WOMEN PHOTOGRAPHERS, C/O Photographics Unlimited, 17 West 17 St., NY, NY 10011. Tel: (212) 726-8292. Educates, supports, and encourages the work of women photographers of all concentrations including photojournalists, fine art photographers, freelance photographers, educators, and individuals who work in industries that support photography. Presents exhibitions and workshops. Publishes a newsletter.

P.S. 1 MUSEUM, THE INSTITUTE FOR CONTEMPORARY ART, 22-25 Jackson Ave., Long Island City, NY 11101. Tel: (718) 784-2084. Functions as a gallery space for art which would not be shown in commercial venues. Offers the Studio Space Program, an international and national program, with free, non-residential, studio spaces for approximately 20 artists for one year.

THE PUBLIC ART FUND, 1 East 53 St., 11th floor, NY, NY 10022. Tel: (212) 980-4575. Fax: (212) 980-3610. Integrates contemporary art within the urban landscape by bringing together artists, communities and city agencies. Provides artists with an opportunity to create art outside the traditional context of museums and galleries, exposing diverse audiences to art in public spaces throughout NYC.

THE PUFFIN FOUNDATION, LTD., 20 East Oakdene Ave., Teaneck, NJ 07666-4198. Awards grants to artists of all disciplines, including art, dance, literature, music, photography, film, and video. Applications are issued in October, November and December. Operates an exhibition space, The Puffin Room, 435 Broome St., 10013. Tel: (212) 343-2881. Fax: (212) 431-4319.

QUEENS COUNCIL ON THE ARTS Oak Ridge at Forest Park, One Forest Park, Woodhaven, New York 11421-1166. Tel: (718) 647-3377 Fax: (718) 647-5036. Email: qca @artswire.org. Supports, promotes, and develops the arts in Queens County. Assists arts organizations and individual artists and presents its diverse cultural resources to the two million residents of the borough, to residents of other boroughs, and to visitors to NYC.

ROCKAWAY ARTISTS ALLIANCE, 118-12 Newport Avenue, Rockaway Park, NY 11694. Tel: (718) 634-6998. Fax: (718) 634-3877. President: Geoff Rawling. A diverse group of artists and art lovers, most of whom live and work in the Rockaways. Enriches the local community by promoting culture and the arts, informing the community of its own unique population of artists, and creating interest in the process of creating art.

THE SALMAGUNDI CLUB, A Center For American Art, 47 Fifth Ave., 10003. Tel: (212) 255-7740. Fax: (212) 229-0172. Advances art in all media, aids artists in exhibiting their work, and helps emerging artists present their work in a professional gallery. All styles, but predominantly representational, in all media. Presents auctions, non-members' shows, and non-juried and juried members' shows.

SALUTE TO WOMEN IN THE ARTS, 120-A Pleasant Avenue, Upper Saddle River, NJ 07458. Tel: (201) 934-6432. An organization of male and female artists in the New Jersey/New York metropolitan area. President: Gloria Duzoglou. Recognizes, supports and "salutes" women in the arts. Helps to create an environment that fosters self expression and creativity through exhibitions, media exposure, career counseling and workshops.

SOCIETY OF ILLUSTRATORS, 128 East 63rd Street, New York, NY 10021. Tel: (212) 838-2560. An international organization of illustrators, photographers, art directors. Maintains a gallery. Publishes an annual book on the best in illustration.

U.S. COPYRIGHT OFFICE. Register of copyrights. The Library of Congress, Washington, DC 20559. Free copyright information kit, containing registration forms for fine artists and other information. For forms call: (202) 707-9100. For information pertaining to copyright law or procedures call: (202) 707-3000.

VOLUNTEER LAWYERS FOR THE ARTS, 1 E. 53 Street, New York, NY 10022. Tel: (212) 319-2787. Arts-related assistance to low-income artists. Art Law Line provides artists with quick answers to arts-related legal questions. Conducts regular seminars on copyright.

WAVE HILL GLYNDOR, 675 West 252 Street, Bronx, 10471. Tel: (718) 549-3200. Fax: (718) 884-8952. Email: info@wavehill.org. URL: http://www.wavehill.org. Presents contemporary artists in all fields whose work explores, demonstrates, or otherwise reflects upon the dynamic relationship between human beings and natural phenomenon.

THE WESTERN STATES ARTS FEDERATION (WESTAF), 1543 Champa St., Suite 220, Denver, CO 80202. Tel: (303) 629-1166. Fax: (303) 629-9717. Email: staff@ westaf.org. Creative advancement and preservation of the arts. Serves the state arts agencies, arts organizations and artists of the West. Engages in innovative approaches to the provision of programs and services. Focuses on strengthening the financial, organizational, and policy infrastructure of the arts in the West. Committed to programmatic activity in the areas of literature, visual arts, American Indian culture, and the folk arts.

THE WESTSIDE ARTS COALITION, Box 527, Cathedral Station, 10025. Tel: (212) 316-6024, (days) or Mr. Tannenbaum (212) 799-4212 (evenings). Organization of visual and performing arts, concerned with helping as many artists as possible. Visual artists join without being juried, however, some exhibitions are juried individually. Maintains gallery at Broadway Mall Community Center, 96th St. and Broadway.

CATHARINE LORILLARD WOLFE ART CLUB, INC., 802 Broadway, New York, NY 10003. An organization of women artists with membership exhibitions and an annual non-member exhibition that offers a variety of awards. Open to all artists with professional quality work, regardless of residence and age. Founder, Catharine Lorillard Wolfe, was among the founders of the Metropolitan Museum of Art.

WOMEN'S CAUCUS FOR ART/ New York Chapter (WCA), #20-B, 340 W. 28th St., NY, NY 10001. A membership organization that provides information and support of women artists. Holds annual conferences, distributes a newsletter and maintains a slide registry and resource file for its members.

THE WORLD STUDIO FOUNDATION 225 Varick Street, 9th floor, New York, NY 10014. Tel: (212) 366-1317. URL:http://www. worldstudio.org. Gives scholarships of between $500 and $2,500 to minority and economically disadvantaged students of an array of visual disciplines.

APPENDIX 3

Recommended Books

303 Marketing Tips: Guaranteed to Boost Your Business by Rieva Lesonsky and Leann Anderson. Published by Entrepreneur.

365 Ways to Simplify Your Work Life by Odette Pollar. Published by Dearborn.

1999 Artist's and Graphic Designer's Market edited by Mary Cox. Published by F & W.

1999 Photographer's Market: 2,000 Places to Sell Your Photographs edited by Megan Lane. Published by F & W.

The A-Z of Art: The World's Greatest & Most Popular Artists & Their Works by Nicola Hodge and Libby Anson. Published by Advanced Marketing Services, Inc.

A Guide to Art: A Handy Reference to Artists, Their Works, and Artistic Movements by Sandro Sproccati. Published by Abrams.

And I Quote compiled by Ashton Appewhite, William R. Evans III, and Andrew Frothingham. Published by St. Martin's Press.

Annual Artists Resource Directory published by Art Calendar.

Art and Its Histories: A Reader by Steve Edwards. Published by Yale University Press.

Art and Photography by Aaron Scharf. Published by Viking Penguin.

Art and Reality: The New Standard Reference Guide and Business Plan for Actively Developing Your Career as an Artist by Robert J. Abbott. Published by Seven Lock.

The ArtFair SourceBook: The Definitive Guide to Fine Art & Contemporary Craft Shows in the United States published by Sourcebook Publishing Company.

Art Information and the Internet: How to Find It, How to Use It by Lois Swan Jones. Published by Onyx Press.

Artists and Writers Colonies published by Blue Heron Press.

Artists' Communities Directory published by The Alliance of Artists' Communities, Portland, Oregon.

Artist to Artist: Inspiration and Advice from Artists Past and Present compiled by Clint Brown. Published by Jackson Creek Press.

The Artist-Gallery Partnership: A Practical Guide To Consigning Art, by Tad Crawford and Susan Mellon. Published by Allworth Press.

The Artist's Friendly Legal Guide by Floyd Conner et al. Published by North Light Books.

The Artist's Guide To New Markets: Opportunities To Show And Sell Art Beyond Galleries by Peggy Hadden. Published by Allworth Press.

The Artist's Resource Handbook by Daniel Grant. Published by Allworth Press.

The Artist's Survival Manual: A Complete Guide To Marketing Your Work by Toby Judith Klayman. Published by Charles Scribner's Sons.

The Artist's Way: *A Spiritual Path to Higher Creativity* by Julia Cameron. Published by Tarcher/Pedigree Books.

Art Law: *The Guide For Collectors, Investors, Dealers, And Artists,* by Ralph E. Lerner and Judith Bresler. Published by Practicing Law Institute.

Art Marketing Handbook: *Marketing Art in the Nineties* by Calvin J. Goodman and Florence J. Goodman. Published by Gee Tee Be.

Art Marketing 101: *A Handbook For The Fine Artist,* by Constance Smith. Published by Art Network.

Art Marketing Sourcebook *3rd Edition, Where to Sell Your Artwork, 2,000 listings* compiled and published by ArtNetwork.

Art Office: *Business Forms, Charts, Sample Letters, Legal Documents & Business Plans For Fine Artists,* by Constance Smith and Sue Viders. Published by ArtNetwork.

Artspeak by Robert Atkins. Published by Abbeyville Press.

Arts Wire Web Manual published by New York Foundation for the Arts. (212) 366-6900.

The Business Of Art edited by Lee Caplin. Published by Prentice-Hall.

Business And Legal Forms For Fine Artists by Tad Crawford. Published by Allworth Press.

Business And Legal Forms For Photographers by Tad Crawford. Published by Allworth Press.

The Business Of Being An Artist, by Daniel Grant. Published by Allworth Press.

The Complete Idiot's Guide to Starting Your Own Business by Ed Paulson and Marcia Layton. Published by Macmillan Publishing Co.

The Concise Oxford Dictionary of Art and Artists by Ian Chilvers. Published by Oxford University Press, Inc.

The CraftFair SourceBook The Definitive Guide to Traditional and Country Craft Shows in the United States. Published by Sourcebook Publishing Company.

The Crafts Supply SourceBook: *A Comprehensive Shop-by-Mail Guide for Thousands of Craft Materials* by Margaret Ann Boyd. Published by F & W.

Chronicles of Courage: Very Special Artists by Jean Kennedy Smith and George Plimpton. Foreword by Robert Coles. Published by Random House.

Everything's Organized by Lisa Kanarek. Published by Career Press, Inc.

Finding Your Perfect Work: *The New Career Guide to Making a Living, Creating a Life* by Paul Edwards and Sarah Edwards. Published by Putnam Publishing Group.

Fine Art Publicity: *The Complete Guide For Galleries And Artists* by Susan Abbott and Barbara Webb. Published by the Art Business News Library.

The Fine Artist's Career Guide by Daniel Grant. Published by Allworth Press.

The Fine Artist's Guide To Marketing And Self-Promotion by Julius Vitali. Published by Allworth Press.

The Fine Artist's Guide To Showing And Selling Your Work by Sally Prince Davis. Published by North Light Books.

Foundry Guide & Directory An A to Z Comparison of 100 Foundries Published by International Sculpture Center.

Go Wild! Creative Opportunities for Artists in the Out-of-Doors compiled by Bonnie Fournier. Published by Lucky Dog Multi-Media.

Grant-Searching Simplified by S.B. Wolfe. Published by Creative Resources, Clyde, NC.

Herstory: Women Who Changed The World by Ruth Ashby and Deborah Gore Ohrn. Introduction by Gloria Steinem. Published by Viking.

How to Get Started Selling Your Art by Carole Katchen. Published by F & W.

How to Handle 1,000 Things at Once: A Fun Guide to Mastering Home & Personal Management by Don Aslett. Published by Marsh Cree.

How To Photograph Paintings by Nat Bukar. Published by ECB Publishing.

How To Photograph Your Art by Malcolm Lubliner. Published by Pomegranate Press.

How To Photograph Your Artwork by Kim Brown. Published by Canyonwinds.

How To Start And Succeed As An Artist by Daniel Grant. Published by Allworth Press.

How To Survive And Prosper As An Artist by Caroll Michels. Published by Henry Holt and Company.

Inside The Art world: Conversations With Barbaralee Diamonstein published by Rizzoli.

Legal Guide For The Visual Artist by Tad Crawford. Published By Allworth Press.

Making Money with Your Creative Paint Finishes by Lynette Harris. Published by F & W.

Marketing Made Easier: Guide To Free Organizing Artists published by National Association of Artists' Organizations.

The McGraw-Hill Guide to Starting Your Own Business: A Step-by-Step Blueprint for the First-Time Entrepreneur by Stephen C. Harper. Published by McGraw-Hill.

Money For Visual Artists published by Americans for the Arts with Allworth Press.

New York Contemporary Art Galleries: The Complete Annual Guide, 1999 Third Edition, by Renée Phillips. Published by Manhattan Arts International. (See order form in this book.)

New York Fine Art Resources: The Fine Artist's Complete Guide to NYC by Renée Phillips. Published by Manhattan Arts International. Publication date: Fall 1999.

New York Publicity Outlets published by Public Relations Plus, Inc.

The Overwhelmed Person's Guide to Time Management by Ronnie Eisenberg. Published by NAL/Dutton.

The Oxford Dictionary of Art edited by Ian Chilvers, Harold Osborne, and Dennis Farr. Published by Oxford University Press.

Photographing Your Artwork: A Step-By-Step Guide To Taking High Quality Slides At An Affordable Price by Russell Hart. Published by North Light.

The Positive Principle Today by Norman Vincent Peale. Published by Fawcett Book Group.

Presentation Power Tools For Fine Artists: *Step-by-Step Professional Advice & Samples* by Renée Phillips. Published by Manhattan Arts. *(See order form in this book.)*

Professional's Guide To Publicity by Richard Winer. Published by Public Relations Publishing Co.

The Prophet, by Kahlil Gibran. Published by Alfred A. Knopf, Inc.

The Publicity Manual by Kate Kelly. Published by Visibility Enterprises.

Restoration of Paintings by Knut Nicolaus. Published by Könemann.

The Road Less Traveled, by M. Scott Peck, MD. Published by Simon & Schuster.

The Seven Habits of Highly Effective People by Stephen R. Covey. Published by Simon & Schuster.

The Seven Spiritual Laws of Success: *A Practical Guide to the Fulfillment of Your Dreams* by Deepak Chopra. Published by Amber-Allen Pubishing and New World Library.

Small Business for Dummies by Eric Tyson and Jim Schell. Published by IDG Books Worldwide.

Taking The Leap: *The Insider's Guide To Exhibiting And Selling Your Art*, By Cay Lang. Published by Chronicle Books.

The Thames and Hudson Dictionary of Art Terms (World of Art), by Edward Lucie-Smith. Published by Thames & Hudson.

Time Management For Busy People by Roberta Roesch. Published by McGraw-Hill Companies, Inc.

Time Management For The Creative Person by Lee Silber. Published by Three Rivers Press.

Time Management for Dummies by Jeffrey J. Mayer. Published by IDG Books Worldwide.

Ulrich's International Periodicals Directory published by R.R. Bowker.

Unstoppable: *45 Powerful Stories Of Perseverance And Triumph From People Just Like You* by Cynthia Kersey. Published by Sourcebooks, Inc.

A Visual Artists Guide to Estate Planning, published by the Marie Walsh Sharpe Foundation and the Judith Rothschild Foundation. Tel: (719) 635-3220.

Wage Slave No More!: *Law And Taxes For The Self-Employed* by Stephen Fishman. Published by Nolo Press.

Working Mothers 101: *How To Organize Your Life, Your Children, And Your Career To Stop Feeling Guilty And Start Enjoying It All* by Katherine Wyse Goldman. Published by HarperCollins.

Working Smart: *How to Accomplish More in Half the Time* by Michael LeBoeuf. Published by Warner Brooks, Inc.

Working Solo: *The Real Guide to Freedom and Financial Success with Your Own Business*, by Terri Lonier. Published by John Wiley & Sons, Inc.

Young Millionaires: *Inspiring Stories To Ignite Your Entrepreneurial Dreams* by Rieva Lesonsky and Gayle Sato Stodder. Published by Entrepreneur Media.

The Zen of Creative Painting by Jeanne Carbonetti. Published by Watson-Guptil.

APPENDIX 4

Recommended Periodicals

Afterimage, 31 Prince Street Rochester, NY 14607. Tel: (716) 442-8676. This bi-monthly magazine covers photography, video, and film.

American Artist, 1515 Broadway, New York, NY 10036. Art magazine published monthly with technical information relating to the visual artists. Offers comprehensive listings of international juried competitions/exhibitions.

Aperture, 20 East 23rd Street New York, NY 10010. This is a quarterly publication on photography.

Art And Auction, 440 Park Avenue South, New York, NY 10016. Art magazine published monthly.

Art Business News, 60 Ridgeway Plaza, Stamford, CT 06905. (213) 356-1745. Art business magazine published monthly. Subscriptions are free to artists.

Artforum, 65 Bleecker Street, New York, NY 10012. Art magazine published monthly.

Art In America, 575 Broadway, New York, NY 10012. Tel: (212) 941-2806. Art magazine published monthly.

Art In America Guide To Museums, Galleries & Artists published in August by *Art in America.*

Artist Call Published by Manchester Publishing, P.O. Box 4468, South Colby, WA 98384-0468. Tel: (360) 871-5371. Fax: (360) 871-5379. E-mail: zuzu@best.com. A monthly newsletter designed to provide visual artists working in all media with a comprehensive resource for current opportunities in the arts.

The Artist's Magazine, 1507 Dana Avenue, Cincinnati, OH 45207. Art magazine geared to the needs of the practicing artist, published monthly.

Art Calendar: The Business Magazine for Visual Artists, PO Box 199, Upper Fairmount, MD 21867-0199. Tel: (410) 651-9150. Publisher: Barbara Dougherty. A monthly magazine that features a range of articles on the business of art and listings of opportunities, fairs and expositions, juried shows.

Art Deadlines List, Resources, Box 381067, Cambridge MA 02238. A monthly resource list of competitions, scholarships, casting calls, calls for visual artists, grants, fellowships, jobs, internships, poetry and other writing contests, financial aid and other art career-related information. Available in paper and by email. A sample listing is available at their website: www.xensei.com/adl/

Art New England: A Resource for Visual Artists, 425 Washington Street, Brighton, MA 02135. Published monthly.

ARTNews, LIC, 48 West 38 Street, New York, NY 10018. (800) 284-4625. An art magazine published monthly.

Art Now Gallery Guide, 97 Grayrock Rd., PO Box 5541, Clinton, NJ 08809. Tel: (908) 638-5255. URL: http://www. galleryguide.com. A monthly guide that lists current exhibitions. Available in the state edition or International Edition.

Artsjobs Free subscription service that posts job opportunities on its website at www.onelist.com/ subscribe.cgi/ARTJOBS.

Art Source Quarterly, published by ArtNetwork, PO Box 1268, Penn Valley, CA 95946. Tel: (530) 470-0862. Fax: (530) 470-0256. Email: info@artmarketing.com URL: http://www.artmarketing.com. A quarterly newsletter that offers artists advice and resources for marketing their work.

Art Times, CSS Publications, Inc., PO Box 730, Mt. Marion, NY 12456. Tel: (914) 246-6944. A monthly publication that provides commentary and resources for all the arts.

Art Trends Magazine: The Magazine of Fine Art Prints, 225 Gordons Corner Road, PO Box 420 Manapalan, NJ 07726. Tel: (800) 969-7176. Fax: (732) 446-5488 General e-mail: info@arttrends.com Website: www.artrends.com

Artweek, 2149 Paragon Drive, Suite 100, San Jose, CA 95131. Tel: (408) 441-7065. In California: (800) 733-2916. This is a weekly publication that covers contemporary fine art on the West Coast.

Artworld Hotline, published by ArtNetwork, PO Box 1268, Penn Valley, CA 95946. Tel: (530) 470-0862. Fax: (530) 470-0256. Email: info@artmarketing.com. URL: http://www.artmarketing.com. A monthly newsletter with listings to advance the artist's career.

Decor: *The Business Magazine of Fine Art and Framing,* 330 North Fourth Street, St. Louis, MO. Tel: (314) 421-5445.

Digital Fine Art magazine, PO Box 420, Manalapan, NJ 07726. A magazine that covers all aspects of digital fine art.

Entrepreneur: The Small Business Authority, Subscriptions: (800) 274-6229. Email: subscribe@entrepreneurmag.com. URL:http://www.entrepreneurmag.com

Flash Art International, Giancarlo Politi Editore, 68 Via Carlo Farini, 20159 Milan, Italy. For subscriptions contact: European Publications, 799 Broadway, New York, NY 10003.

F.Y.I., published by Foundation for the Arts, 155 Avenue of the Americas, New York, NY 10013. A newsletter that contains vital information for performing and visual artists. *(For more information about the organization see Appendix 2.)*

Manhattan Arts International, 200 East 72 St., Suite 26L, New York, NY 10021. Tel: (212) 472-1660. A bimonthly magazine that features essays on arts issues, profiles and interviews with emerging and established artists and art dealers, and previews/reviews of exhibitions. Contains *Success Now! For Artists,* an 8-page supplement that offers advice and opportunities for artists. *(See order form in this book.)*

New Art Examiner, 314 West Institute Place, Chicago, IL 60610. This monthly magazine contains in-depth discussions of current art issues as well as exhibition coverage.

The Newsletter published by Caroll Michels, 19 Springwood Lane, East Hampton, New York 11937. Tel: (516) 329-9105. Fax: (516) 329-9107. Email: Carollmich@aol.com. A monthly newsletter with resources and opportunities for fine artists. Caroll Michels is a coach/artist advocate. She is also the author of *How to Survive & Prosper as an Artist.*

New York Publicity Outlets, Published by Public Relations Plus, Inc., PO Box 1197, New Milford, CT 06776. Tel: (800) 999-8448. A resource book published every six months.

Photography in New York International, 64 West 89 Street, #3F, New York, NY 10025. A bi-monthly guide to current photography exhibitions in New York. Also lists private dealers.

The Photo Review, 301 Hill Avenue, Langhorne, PA 19047. A monthly newsletter with complete listings of photography exhibitions throughout the Mid-Atlantic region.

Picture Framing Magazine, 225 Gordons Corner Rd/ PO Box 420 Manalapan NJ 07726. www.pictureframe.com. An industry magazine that features all aspects of the picture framing business, from technical how-to articles to trends and creative ideas. Their website will lead you to local framers.

Sculpture **Magazine,** Published by the International Sculpture Center, a nonprofit membership organization. Tel: (212) 785-1144. The only international publication devoted exclusively to contemporary sculpture. It features criticism, reviews, studio visits, interviews, technical information, and timely listings of commissions, calls for artists, grants, residencies, and workshops.

Sculpture Review, published by the National Sculpture Society, 1177 Avenue of the Americas, New York, NY 10036. Tel: (212) 764-5645. A quarterly magazine that covers timely topics related to sculpture. It is one of the benefits of membership with the National Sculpture Society.

StudioNOTES, Box 502, Benicia, CA 94510. Tel: (707) 746-5516. Email: snotes1@ix.netcom.com. A monthly newsletter with ideas and information for artists, with an emphasis on subscribers sharing their ideas and viewpoints and experiences with each other.

Success Now! The Artrepreneur Newsletter for Fine Artists published by Manhattan Arts International. A monthly newsletter with how-to information, career advice, and listings of opportunities for exhibitions, sales and promotion. Available as a supplement in *Manhattan Arts International* magazine six times a year, plus four separate issues. Tel: (212) 472-1660. *(See order form in this book.)*

Index

A
accountants, 158
advertising/advertisements
   alternatives to, 175, 177
   bartering for, 169
   of competitions, 128-129
   galleries, 46, 57, 58
   as part of goal setting, 124
   part of marketing, 146,149,151
   usage, 150, 151
advocacy/advocates, 16, 92, 146, 177, see also Appendix 2
A.I.R. Gallery, 86
Alda, Alan, 13
The Alternative Museum, 128
alternative space(s), 9, 16, 41, 44, 55,125,146, see also Appendix 2
American Music Awards, 182
American Society of Contemporary Artists, 4, 9, 12, 44, 198
American Society of Interior Designers, 151
American Watercolor Society, 44, 146, 199
animal portraits, 146
Annonymous Was A Woman, 90
Archaic and Classical Greek Art, 143
architects/architectural firms, 57, 146, 151, 154, 155, 158, 197, 198, 199, 201, 203
art brut, 157
Art Calendar, 78, 130, 208, 212
"Art Chicago", 157
art consultant(s),
   artists' relationship to, 32, 49,
   corporate sales, 116, 154
   galleries' relationship to, 57
   locating, 153
   marketing art, 146, 158
Art Dealers Association of America (ADAA), 157, 199
Art Editions, 162
art fairs/expositions, 156-157, 173
Art Expo, 156, 157

The Art Fair Sourcebook, 157, 208
Artforum, 45, 176, 212
The Artful Traveler, 182
art, the healing power of/healing art, 23, 134, 145, 147, 160, 182, 192-193
Art in America, 45
Art in America Annual Guide to Museums, Galleries, Artists, 45
Art Information Center, 42, 199
Art in General, 44, 199
The Artist's Proof, 9, 12, 204
artist's statement, 187, 191
"Artists: How to Break into New York Galleries", 9, 38
Artists Space, 154, 199
Artists Talk on Art, 4, 9,78, 200
art market
   changes over decades, 171
   pursuit of, 145, 173
   see also marketing
Art Marketing 101, 151, 209
Art Marketing Sourcebook, 151
ArtNetwork, 151
ARTnews, 45, 148, 212
ARTnews International Directory of Corporate Art Collections, 153
Artopia, 16, 81
The Art Show, 157, 199
Art Trends: The Magazine of Fine Art Prints, 172, 213
art/artist organization(s),
   for beginner artists, 44
   competitions, 128
   power and importance of, 78-81
   sharing tasks, 103
   as volunteer for, 75, 80
   women's, 80, 87
art world
   artist's influence upon, 19-20
   artist's position in, 66, 69, 72, 75
   harsh realities of, 30, 32
   discrimination in, 87-88
Association of Art Museum Directors, 89

Association of International Photography Art Dealers (AIPAD), 157
Attorney General/Attorney General's Office, 51, 56, 129
awards/fellowships
   for building confidence, 26, 61
   as goals, 118
   juried competitions, 125, 126
   publicity for, 177
   and value of art, 162, 163,167
   women, 86, 90
   see also Appendix 2

B
Bacon, Francis, 102
bank(s)
   exhibiting in, 44, 140, 151, 158, 185
bank account, 136
bankruptcy, 39, 62, 98
Barnes & Noble, 183
barter, 116, 169
Bascom, Joe, 127
Beda, Gaye Elise, 4, 167
Benglis, Lynda, 176
Better Business Bureau, 51, 129, 130, 184
biography, 115, 162
body of work
   focus, 22, 66, 195
   and galleries, 47
   marketing, 95, 145
Boorstein, Daniel J., 175
botanical associations, 147, 158
Brihadaranyaka Uypanishad, 12
brochure(s),
   in galleries, 52
   artists' sales, 48, 54, 116, 150, 151, 162, 173
Broome Street Gallery, 52, 204
budget, 93, 96, 98, 123, 179
Burnett, Leo, 169
Burr Artists, 44, 200
business of art
   artists' relationship to, 92
   and coach, 83
   and dealers, 136
   and money, 114
   learning, 15, 29, 30-34, 186, 195
   taking care of, 91-106
   and women, 90
business card, 74, 150

business plan, 113, 124, see also Appendix 3
   part of marketing, 144
Business and Legal Forms for Fine Artists, 51, 209
buyers
   attaining, 55, 124, 146-154, 160-166, 195
   attitude of, 136, 174
   changes of, 92
   and galleries, 47, 52, 57
   keeping, 170, 171
   and prices, 173
   relationship to, 49
buying art, resistance to, 171

C
Cacciola, J., 48
calendar(s)
   creating/marketing, 146, 168
   editorial, 182
   use of, 101, 103, 165
camaraderie, 31, 72, 77-81, 149
Carnegie, Dale, 34
cash flow, 14, 97-98, 113, 117, 196
Cassatt, Mary, 88, 125
Castelli Gallery, Leo, 136
CD-Roms, 47, 154
Ceres Gallery, 86
Chelsea
   New York, 19
   London's, 20
Chicago, Judy, 85, 88, 90, 92
children's portraits, 146
Chamber(s) of Commerce, 130, 149, 158, 181, 184, 185
charity(ies), 75, 149, 158, 166, 168, 178, 183-185
Churchill, Winston, 139
Close, Chuck 18, 21, 62
coach, career, 9, 16, 17, 82-83, 104, 196
Coca-Cola, 66
Cocteau, Jean, 187
Color Card, 162
Color Q, 162
commitment, 62-64
   gallery's, 39, 53, 139
   to a gallery, 49
   and goals, 112, 119, 152
   importance of, 41, 43, 59, 80, 95, 180, 196

communication, 15
    importance of, 160, 187-191
    internet, 79
    non-verbal, 189
    verbal and written, 48, 51, 139
communications director, 153
competition, 30
competitions,
    and the beginning artist, 44
    and discrimination, 87
    galleries, 57
    juried, 125-135
    Manhattan Arts, 136, 182
    part of marketing plan, 137, 158
    and rejection, 136
    and value of art, 37, 113
computer
    for artist's newsletter, 167
    CD-Roms, 154
    and creativity, 20, 168
    interest group, 183
    for maintenance of mailing list/contacts, 74, 101, 104
    as time-saver, 78, 102,
Concholar, Dan, 43, 199
confidence, 26, 36, 99
    importance of, 59-60
    and galleries, 43, 48
    and relationships, 77
    and selling, 160-171
    see also rejection
consistency of style, 47
consulate(s), 158, 181
contract
    with gallery, 39, 50, 51, 53, 54, 56, 57, 196
    and renting art, 169
copyright, 196, 207
corporations, 96, 136, 152-155, 158
cover letter, 46, 96, 139
Crain's New York Business, 9, 151
Crawford, Tad, 51, 208
creative blocks, 84
"Creativity / Creative Process Groups", 84
Crisp, Quentin, 38
critic(s), 10, 203
    artist as, 72
    artist relationship with, 31, 48, 72, 75, 80, 149, 187
    as competition juror, 127, 128, 131
    discrimination, 87
    influence on dealers, 54
    as profession, 20
    publicity, 179
    rejection by, 132, 134, 136
    roles of, 72
    value of art, 162
criticism, 31, 74, 195
"cross-promotion", 178
curator(s),
    artist as, 75
    artist relationship with, 75, 80, 149
    communication with, 186
    as competition juror, 115, 127,
    influence on dealers, 48
    interchanging roles, 72
    as profession, 20
    use of slide registries, 49
customer, 33, 79, 116, 160, 163-168
customer profile, 147-150

D
Dali, 34
Darwin, Charles, 119
David, Jacques-Louis, 145
de Goya, Francisco, 157
dealers. See also galleries.
    C-D Roms, 154
    demands, 24
    discrimination, 86
    interests/tastes, 27, 45-48, 125, 136, 139
    myths about New York, 31, 42
    artist relationship with, 39, 72, 75, 80, 116, 166, 187, 188
    rejection by, 137
    relationship with buyers, 92, 161, 171
    vanity galleries, 54
Degas, Edgar, 159
demonstration(s), art, 146, 166, 181, 185
Dinkins, David, 9, 186
derivative, 21
De Chirico, Giorgio, 25
Dickinson's *1998 Statistical Survey of Gender Discrimination in the Visual Art Field*, Eleanor, 86
digital prints, 47, 172

INDEX 217

Digital Fine Art, 172, 213
Dr. Seuss, 66
Dubuffet, Jean, 136
Duchamp, Marcel, 76
Durand, Asher B., 161
Dylan, Bob, 17

E
Edison, Thomas A., 138
Emerson, Ralph Waldo, 30, 81, 92
entrepreneur(s), 33, 91, 92, 97
Entrepreneur, 162, 206, 213
Epicurus, 73
Epstein, Jacob, 175
exhibition(s)
   See also juried competitions.
   alternative space, 140, 146, 168
   artist curated, 92, 122
   in New York, 41-51
   lapses between, 88
   paying for, 53-57, 156, 174
   selling at, 165-166
   through organizations, 77, 78, 80, 81
   timing for, 181, 182

F
fairs/expositions, 156-157, 158, 173.
   See also Appendix 2.
feng shui, 155
Feuerman, Carole A., 167
Fine Art Iris Prints, 172
Flaubert, Gustave, 177
Fosdick, Dr. Harry Emerson, 117
The Foundation Center, 130
Fowler, Gene, 190
Franklin, Benjamin, 73
Franklin Mint, 146, 158
Frost, Robert, 66
Fusion-Arts Review, 16
Futurism, 175

G
galleries
   alternatives to, 140-141
   cooperative, 44, 52, 55, 77, 127, 128
   fee-paid, 51-58
   New York, 22, 38-58
Gallery 84, 127
Gallery Guide, 45, 212
Gallery Henoch, 45
Gannet Transit, 177
Giclée, 172

Giordano, Joan, 189
Giotto, 91
goals, 13, 14, 59, 110-122
   commitment to, 62, 64, 67, 69
   career, 110-112, 123
   help of coach, 82, 83
   financial, 96, 113-116, 124, 164
   long-term, 34
   of group/organization, 80, 81, 82
   visualization of, 117, 118
Goethe, 62
Greek Art and Culture, 181
Greek potters, 143
Greene, Marlena, 49
Guerrilla Girls, 90

H
Hamptons, 20, 33
handouts, 74, 181, 195
Haring, Keith, 176
Hayes, Helen, 32
Hayes, James L., 79
The Heart of the Question, 87
Heller Gallery, 41
Henri, Robert, 180
Hermel, Sidney H., 4, 65, 205
Hill, Napoleon, 34
History of Modern Art, 87
Hoffman, Nancy, 43
How to Survive & Prosper as an Artist, 153, 210, 213
Huxley, Aldous, 118

I
Images Gallery, 49
Indig, Sandra, 84
International Sculpture Center, 146, 203, 210, 214
interior designers, 57, 146, 147, 154, 158
intuitive art, 157
InvestinArt, 49, 136
Iris prints, 172

J
Jacob Javits Convention Center, 156
Janson, H.W., 87
journal
   of expenses, 98
   communication tool, 31, 191-192
juried competitions/exhibitions, 26, 44, 87, 115, 125-131, 158
   entry fees, 128, 130

jurors' fees, 128-129
K
Kahlo, Frida, 21, 88, 90
Kandinsky, Vasilly, 28
Karp, Ivan, 40
Keller, Helen, 14, 33, 141
Kennedy, John F., 19, 80
Kertess, Klaus, 139, 140
Koons, Jeff, 176
Krasner, Lee, 63
Kuspit, Donald, 127
L
Lambert, Eleanor, 175
legal, 51, 169
Letters to the Editor, 180
Lichtenstein, Roy, 192
Lonier, Terri, 98
M
mailing list, 48, 53, 56, 167, 174
 building, 149, 150-151, 195
 organizing, 98,101, 104
Mandela, 109
Manhattan Arts International
 about 9, 16
 annual competition, 136
 events, 90, 181-183
 marketing art, 151,
 Salute to Women in the Arts, 92
 source of gallery leads 45,
 writers for, 75
market, 143-158
 corporate, 153-155
 identifying, 145-147
 venues, 158
marketing
 about, 143-144
 history, 143
market niche, 145, 152
market research, 173
Matisse, Henri, 27, 34
Marsalis, Wynton, 182
Marxer, Donna, 4, 78, 200
Max, Peter, 176
Meat Market Crawls, 178
Meat Market District, 178
media (press), 9, 54, 66, 179-181, 183
media (medium), 31, 42, 47, 127, 146, 149, 172, 173
 see also Appendix 2.
media campaign, 23

media list, 179
media, mixed, 168, 188
media, multi-, 16, 81
Mendez, Louis, 189
Michels, Caroll, 153, 210, 213
Miller, Henry, 15
minority artists, 127, 207
Minter, Marilyn, 176
Mitchell Graphics, 162
Modern Postcard, 163
Modersohn-Becker, Paula, 24
Monet, 82, 120
Morley, Christopher, 36
More, Thomas, 16
Mother Theresa, 109
Multiple Impressions, Ltd., 47
multiples, 47
Munch, Edvard, 20
museum(s)
 See also curators
 See also Appendix 2
 discrimination in, 86-89
 exhibitions in, 125, 130
 varied uses, 34, 149, 181, 183
 as market leads, 96, 144, 146, 152, 158
Museum of Modern Art (MoMA), 128
myths
 about artists, 32-36
 about collectors, 148
 about galleries, 38
 about selling, 160-163
N
National Association of Women Artists, 44, 86, 204
The National Black Fine Art Show, 157
national events, 182
National Museum of Women in the Arts, 86, 89
National Sculpture Society, 44, 214
nautical, 145
Neel, Alice, 23
Network/networking, 72-78
 function of galleries, 58
 to get into galleries, 48
 public relations, 175, 176, 187
 sales, 149
New York Newsday, 9, 177
The Newsletter, 153, 213

newsletter(s),
  see also Appendix 2
  art organizations, 79, 81, 123,
  artist's, 167
  as resources, Appendix 4
New York Artists Equity Association, 4, 9, 16, 52, 80, 128, 186, 204
New York Contemporary Art Galleries, 4, 9, 42, 45, 210
  galleries' selection process, 72
  women artists in, 85
  women dealers in, 85
New York Society of Women Artists, 4, 9, 44, 86, 205

O
Ohio State Arts Council, 78
O'Keefe, Georgia, 22, 88
Open Studio, 142, 150, 158, 165, 169
Organization of Independent Artists, 78, 205
Osborne, Robin, 143
The Outsider Art Fair, 157
Oxford University Press, 143, 209, 210

P
Parsons, Betty, 143
The Pastel Society, 4, 44, 65, 146
Pauling, Linus, 172
Peale, Norman Vincent, 34
Pen & Brush Club, 86, 205
perfectionism, 120
Pernod, 128
Photo CDs, 154
The Photography Show, 157
Picasso, Pablo, 34
Pindell, Howardena, 87
Plimpton, George, 62
Pollock, Jackson, 175
positive affirmations, 118
Post Script Press, 162
presentation materials, 110, 115, 144, 162, 196
  gallery, 46
press kit, 180
promotional/sales materials, 66, 101, 162, 163, 169, 195
Presentation Power Tools, 17, 50, 174, 176
the press
  attracting, 177, 178, 182, 185
  contact with, 80, 81, 166

dealing with, 32, 188
gallery relationship with, 57
press kit, 180
price(s)/pricing, 55, 116
  changes in, 171
  galleries, 42
  raising, 124
  determining, 173-174, 179, 196
Priest, Ivy Baker, 91
prints, 152
  art fairs, 156
  benefits of, 119
  corporations, 154
  digital, 47, 172
  Fine Art Iris, 172
  goals, 124
  laser, 47
  marketing, 147, 152, 155, 168
psychology, 53, 83, 162
psychotherapy, 84
The Puck Building, 157
public relations/publicity, 85, 87, 175-180, 185

Q
"Quarterly Report", 78

R
Rauschenberg, Robert, 136
rejection, 25, 195
  dealing with, 60, 67, 133-142
  from competitions, 127
  from galleries, 39, 43, 137
Renoir, Pierre Auguste, 82
rent art, 169
Resume
  for selling art, 54, 155, 162, 173, 174, 196
  comparative study, 46
  developing, 185
  updating, 98, 104
  lapses in, 90
The Richmond Galleries, 178
Robbins, Anthony, 83
Rodriguez, Geno, 128
role models, 34, 37, 82, 87, 137
Roosevelt, Eleanor, 60
Roosevelt, Theodore, 132
Rose, Roslyn, 188
Rosenberg, Harold, 166
Rubens, 34
Rubin, Edward, 4, 12

S
The Salmagundi Club, 44, 198, 199, 206
Schedule C, 140
Schell, Jim, 98, 211
self-expression, 21-28, 64, 108
self-sabotage, 14, 29-31
self-sufficiency, 34, 38, 60, 114, 195
self-taught, 157
serigraphs, 23
Seventh Regiment Armory, 157, 199
Shakespeare, William, 119
Shane, Corinne, 136
Shaw, George Bernard, 188
Sills, Beverly, 182
slide registry(s), 49, 146, 154,158, 205, 207, 214,
slides, 130-131
 critique, 79
 to galleries, 30, 40, 41, 43, 46, 72, 73
 storage of, 100, 101
Small Business for Dummies,98,211
Smith, Jean Kennedy, 62
social/political, 146
Socrates, 108
SoHo, 19, 49, 52, 56, 128
SoHo 20 Gallery, 86
Sonnabend, Ileana, 149
stereotype(s), 31, 35, 36, 42
Steinbaum Krauss Gallery, 86
Stevenson, Robert Louis, 137, 167
Stewart, Regina, 4, 80
Storr, Robert, 128
Super Bowls, 177
Swetchine, Anne-Sophie, 96

T
time management, 14, 64, 99-104
Tribeca, 19
Tsu, Lao, 95, 107
Twain, Mark, 97
Tyson, Eric, 98, 211
Tzu, Sun, 74

U
universities
 exhibiting in, 44
 as market venue, 158
 statistical data from, 86

 teaching business of art, 92
U.S. Tournament, 177
Utopia, 16

V
vanity galleries, 56, 57
 See also galleries, fee-paid.
Vincent van Gogh, 35, 136
visionary art, 145, 157
visualization, 117-118
volunteer(s)
 arts organizations, 75, 80
 charity, 23
 jurors, 128
 to expand market, 149
 recruiting, 93
 for P.R. success, 183-186
 to help women, 87

W
Warhol, Andy, 151, 176, 178
The Westside Arts Coalition, 44, 207
Whelihan, Anthony, 167
Whitney Biennials, 136
Who's Who Directories, 151, 158
Who's Who in the Latin American Community, 152
Wilde, Oscar, 83, 176
Wilson, Earl, 140
wineries, 158
Catharine Lorillard Wolfe Art Club, 44, 86, 207
Women. See also Appendix 2.
 artists represented by New York galleries, 85
 status of, 85-90
 gallery owners, New York, 85
Women Executives in Public Relations, 85
Women in the Arts, 182
Wood, Beatrice, 34
Woodworth, Fred, 69
Working Solo: The Real Guide to Freedom and Financial Success with Your Own Business, 98, 211
Wyeth, Andrew, 26

Z
Zappa, Frank, 182

RENÉE PHILLIPS
Schedule of Upcoming Workshops

Artists: Break Into New York Galleries
Thursday, June 24   6:30-9:30 PM

A three-hour comprehensive course that reveals the inner workings of the New York City gallery system. Ms. Phillips shows you who, how, when and where to approach for your work. She also offers advice on how to prosper without a gallery. Offered by the Learning Annex, in New York, NY. Reservations are required. Call for reservations, fees and location. (212) 371-0280.

The same course is repeated on

July 28	6:30-9:30 PM	September 16	6:30-9:30 PM
October 20	6:30-9:30 PM	November 18	6:30-9:30 PM

Reach Your Creative Potential and Have Prosperity!
Monday, June 28   6:30-8:30 PM

Renée Phillips will discuss the rich rewards that artists can achieve through a balance of creative fulfillment and financial freedom. Based on 20 years experience counseling artists of all career levels, styles and media. This workshop is free but seating is limited. Arrive promptly. Nexus Gallery, 345 E. 12th St., New York, NY. Tel: (212) 982-4712. For information call (212) 472-1660.

Success Now! For Artists
Monday, September 13   8:00 PM

In this seminar Ms. Phillips will discuss a variety of ways in which artists can take charge of their careers and reach their goals. Sponsored by Rockaway Artists Alliance, at Fort Tilden Chapel, Rockaway Beach, NY. This workshop is free and open to all artists and artists' agents. For more information call Rockaway Artists Alliance (718) 474-0861 or Manhattan Arts (212) 472-1660.

Prosperity! Strategies for the New Millennium
Thursday, September 23   6:30-9:30 PM

Renée Phillips will offer strategies to reach self-sufficiency, through sales of your work, finding markets, arranging Open Studios, developing relationships with corporate art buyers, and dealers, and attracting collectors. Reservations are required. For reservations, fees and location call: (212) 472-1660. (This course is offered regularly.)

Renée Phillips is available to speak at your gallery, artist organization school or bookstore. For additional information about these events and other workshops conducted by Renée Phillips contact

Manhattan Arts
INTERNATIONAL

Tel: (212) 472-1660   Fax: (212) 794-0324   Email: Manarts@aol.com

Comments about Renée Phillips

"Renée Phillips' seminars go straight to the point. She sounds the clarion call for 'self-empowerment' and is the voice of the artist of the *fin de siecle* and the 21st century." **Bernard Olshan, Artist, National Academy Museum, and V.P., American Society of Contemporary Artists**

"Renée Phillips inspires, guides and encourages artists to reach their goals through sound advice on the business of art. Her lectures are standing-room only." **Regina Stewart, Executive Director, NY Artists Equity**

"Everyone felt your talk was the best we have had. Your practical good sense, tremendous amount of research, and genuine understanding of what goes into creating art made for an unusually informative presentation."
Jean T. Kroeber, Catharine Lorillard Wolfe Art Club

"I want to express my thanks to you for serving on the Jury of Awards for the Catharine Lorillard Wolfe Art Club's 101st Annual Exhibit at the National Arts Club. We feel honored to have had you lend your time and expertise toward making our show the success it is." **Nissan Gallant, Painting Chairman**

"I have never met anyone in the art world like Renée Phillips who is so singularly focused in her pursuit to help artists establish and further their careers."
Edward Rubin, NY critic

"Montague Art Gallery was honored to have you present seminars in our gallery. You define the art world in a unique and comprehensive manner. We hope you will schedule more." **Rosemarie Montague**

"I won a $15,000 Pollack-Krasner Grant, thanks to my private consultation with you and your career guidance." **Stephen Alarid**

"On behalf of New York University I wish to convey my gratitude to you for the information you shared. It made a positive impact." **Allen M. McFarlane**

"Your expertise, time and enthusiasm made a most intriguing evening. It's been weeks since your standing-room-only talk and many artists are still excited about the fireworks you created."
Richard Pionk, President, The Salmagundi Club

"I would like to thank you on behalf of everyone at City College who attended your workshop and to have the opportunity to learn from your expertise. We truly appreciated your enthusiasm and generosity as well as the valuable information you shared." **Susan Smolinsky, Graduate Art Society of City College**

"I traveled from San Francisco to attend your workshop. I am so pleased that I made the effort. Thank you for providing the art world with such an informative venue. I have already made progress in several areas as a result of what I learned that evening." **Monica V. Loncola**

"On behalf of the members of Women Executives in Public Relations, I would like to thank you for taking part in the panel discussion on "The Status of Women in the Arts." Your presentation was excellent. We are extremely grateful to you for sharing your knowledge and insight with our group."
Lucy Siegel

"Your advice has given me the courage and the knowledge to communicate with the press and the media with great success. You are a pioneer in your work and your services are greatly appreciated." **Sylvana Soligon**

"I feel that my consultation with you and your articles positioned me well to make a big sale. I thank you for you energy and talent and point of view. Consulting you was a turning point for me." **June Bisantz-Evans**

"I had the pleasure of attending your lecture. I was very encouraged and motivated by your knowledge and ideas. It's encouraging to know that serious artists have someone pulling for them." **Jackie Zaronsky**

"Since I had the consultation with you, it has been much easier to handle my art business. Your tools helped me to receive two awards and my resume has been enhanced. My clients are more interested since I established contact with each of them, in the way you advised. Your referrals are very important to me.
Marie Deras

"I was one of the lucky persons to enroll in one of your workshops, and shortly after I had a private consultation with you. It helped me a great deal; I focused on achieving my goal, a solo show." **Ana Silvia Arias**

"I attended your NY Galleries lecture. I went away from the lecture revitalized, more sensible and better prepared. Bravo! To you and your contagious energy!" **Elizabeth Schippert**

"I took your workshop at Marymount Manhattan College and I am grateful. Thanks so much for your presence and all you've done. I truly appreciate your steadfastness and courage. You are providing a wonderful artist community service." **Cynthia Van Leeuwen**

"The workshop helped me focus on what I need to do now – to move forward. You made the promotional stage seem less daunting!"
Karen Martin

"Your workshop inspired me to think larger in terms of getting my art out into the world." **Mira Fink**

"The workshop was very helpful and supportive. I have always found your *Success Now!* newsletter to be very informative and encouraging. Thank you for your words of wisdom, direction and support." **Joyce Pommer**

THE MOST COMPREHENSIVE DIRECTORY OF ITS KIND

More than 760 Detailed Listings!

COMMERCIAL GALLERIES
NON-PROFIT ORGANIZATIONS
ALTERNATIVE SPACES
PRIVATE DEALERS
MUSEUMS

Each listing includes contact names, address, tel & fax, email, website, hours, role/philosophy, artists shown, description of styles and media, prices, artist selection process, how/when artists should approach them, and more...

Whether you are a student or professional this book offers instructional value on every level. It's an explorer's companion to personal access to the New York Art world as manifested in its exhibition spaces.
**Donna Cameron, Artist, Writer, Filmmaker.
Faculty, Tisch School of the Arts,
New York University and School of Visual Arts.**

For anybody interested in the workings of the art world and the mysteries of the gallery system.
Edward Rubin, New York art critic

No journal better serves the aspiring artist or the tourist confounded by surfeit.
Ivan Karp, Owner & Director, O.K. Harris Gallery, New York, NY

Author: Renée Phillips
$18.95
ISBN 0-9646358-5-2   SEE PAGE 229 FOR ORDERING INFORMATION

SUCCESS NOW! FOR ARTISTS

Manhattan Arts
INTERNATIONAL

A bi-monthly magazine that features behind the scenes profiles of artists, critics, curators and dealers, provocative essays on art issues, insightful articles about the creative process, reviews and previews of current and upcoming exhibitions and events, art website reports, candid photographs of art stars at NYC galas, international art news, art book previews, and much more.

Every issue contains **Success Now!**
The Artrepreneur Newsletter For Fine Artists

An 8-page supplement filled with a wide variety of opportunities, juried shows, resources and advice for artists of all media. Each issue will motivate and direct you to attain your career goals.

With a one-year subscription to **Manhattan Arts International** you'll receive 6 bi-monthly issues of the magazine...
Plus: 4 additional issues of **Success Now!**

Subscription Rates:

United States	1 Year: $30	2 Years: $54
Canada & Mexico	1 Year: $36	2 Years: $65
All Other Countries	1 Year: $45	2 Years: $80
Sample copy: United States $5	All other countries: $8	

SEE PAGE 229 FOR ORDERING INFORMATION

> "The straightforward instructions, copious samples, and helpful tips in all areas of promotion and publicity make up a systematic approach to achieve professional success. This invaluable, well-researched information will help artists help themselves."
> Jen MacDonald, Artist and Editor, *Money For Artists*

PRESENTATION POWER TOOLS FOR FINE ARTISTS

STEP-BY-STEP INSTRUCTIONS
PROFESSIONAL ADVICE
A VARIETY OF SAMPLES

- BUSINESS LETTERS
- RESUMES & BIOGRAPHIES
- ARTIST'S STATEMENTS
- PRESS RELEASES
- PROMOTION PIECES
- ARTIST/GALLERY CHECKLIST
- CERTIFICATE OF AUTHENTICITY
- RESOURCES *AND MORE!*

RENEÉ PHILLIPS

Manhattan Arts
INTERNATIONAL

This book will help you prepare a polished, professional approach to dealers, critics and collectors.

"A very practical resource that offers a glimpse of what other artists are producing... and a great aid in setting up one's own materials."
Constance Smith, Director, ArtNetwork and author *Art Marketing 101*

An important resource for any Fine Art professional engaged in promoting and selling Art. Step-by-step writing guidelines and expert advice are designed to save time, frustration and costly mistakes in the preparation of promotional materials. Actual samples of Business Letters, Resumes, Biographies, Artist's Statements, Promotion Pieces, Comment Sheets and Press Releases are provided. It contains an Artist/Gallery Agreement Checklist and Certificate of Authenticity. The chapter on "The Publicity Campaign" offers expert advice by the author and public relations specialists in the arts. It shows you how to develop a rapport with the media and obtain the recognition you need for increasing the value of your art work.

Author: Renée Phillips
$18.95
ISBN 0-9646358-5-2   SEE PAGE 229 FOR ORDERING INFORMATION

I would like to hear from you!

I hope this book has helped you and
will continue to be a source of career guidance.
If it has I would like to know how.
Please write to me with your comments
as well as your suggestions about
topics to discuss in future books and workshops,
and in *Manhattan Arts International* magazine
Success Now! For Artists newsletter,
and our Manhattan Arts website.

Thank you.

I wish you creative bliss!
Renée Phillips

Manhattan Arts
INTERNATIONAL

200 East 72 Street, Suite 26-L
New York, NY 10021

Email: Manarts@aol.com

ORDER FORM

QTY	ITEM	PRICE	AMOUNT
	*SUCCESS NOW! FOR ARTISTS A MOTIVATIONAL GUIDE	$18.95	
	*PRESENTATION POWER TOOLS FOR FINE ARTISTS	$18.95	
	*NEW YORK CONTEMPORARY ART GALLERIES 1999 EDITION	$18.95	
	MANHATTAN ARTS INTERNATIONAL SUBSCRIPTION		
	U.S.	1 YEAR $30.00	
		2 YEARS $54.00	
	CANADA & MEXICO	1 YEAR $36.00	
		2 YEARS $65.00	
	ALL OTHER COUNTRIES	1 YEAR $45.00	
		2 YEARS $80.00	
	NEW YORK GALLERIES MAILING LIST ON LABELS FROM NY CONTEMPORARY ART GALLERIES (APPROX. 760)		
	UNITED STATES	$63.00	
	ALL OTHER COUNTRIES	$75.00	
		SUBTOTAL	
		SHIPPING *	
		TOTAL	

*SHIPPING/HANDLING CHARGES FOR BOOKS
U.S. Please add for the first book $5.00.
Each additional book please add $2.50.

OTHER COUNTRIES: Please add for the first book $17.00.
Each additional book please add $8.50.

Name_____

Address_____

city _____ state _____

zip_____ Email:_____

Where did you buy this book? _____

☐ Place my name on your mailing list to receive announcements of future books, and workshops and seminars.

PLEASE MAKE CHECK PAYABLE IN U.S. FUNDS FROM A U.S. BANK TO
Manhattan Arts International
200 East 72 Street, New York, NY 10021 Tel: (212) 472-1660
Fax: (212) 794-0324 Email: Manarts@aol.com
(Sorry, no foreign checks or foreign money orders are accepted.)